STAGE II

Integrated  Business Technology

RSA
Examinations Board

Heinemann

Heinemann Educational Publishers
Halley Court, Jordan Hill, Oxford OX2 8EJ
A Division of Reed Educational & Professional Publishing Ltd

MELBOURNE   AUCKLAND
FLORENCE   PRAGUE   MADRID   ATHENS
SINGAPORE   TOKYO   CHICAGO   SAO PAULO
PORTSMOUTH NH   MEXICO
IBADAN   GABORONE   JOHANNESBURG
KAMPALA   NAIROBI

© RSA Examinations Board, 1996

First published 1996

99 98 97
10 9 8 7 6 5 4

British Library Cataloguing in Publication Data
A catalogue record for this book is available from the British Library

ISBN 0 435 45194 4

Designed and typeset by Gecko Ltd, Bicester, Oxon
Cover design by Dennis Fairey & Asc. Ltd, Hertfordshire
Printed and bound in England by Bath Press

Acknowledgements

The author and publishers would like to thank the following for assisting in the
preparation of the text, and also those who assisted in providing the photographs:

Peter Stallman, Stallman Interiors
Norman Southern, Wirral Security Bureau

Fraser Bird for taking the photographs.

It should be noted that although the assignments are designed to reflect the use of
information technology in the above businesses, the data is not drawn from their files,
nor would the reports necessarily be constructed in the manner requested. All data has
been drawn up for the purposes of assessment, and does not depict any real event.

Contents

Foreword

RSA's Integrated Business Technology Stage II (IBTII) scheme was developed to replace Applications of Office Technology Stage II (AOTII). The new scheme tests many of the same applications, but the old scheme did not require the electronic integration of information between applications. RSA considers that it is now appropriate to accredit the use of integrated computer software, which is increasingly found in the business environment.

The scheme is designed to test the practical use of the most common software applications: database, spreadsheet, word processing and graphing programs. These files are then brought together, in the integration assignment, to present a final report based upon the word processed document, but containing electronically integrated extracts from the database, spreadsheet and graphing assignments.

This book contains build up exercises for each of the applications, and a complete set of IBTII specimen assignments. A Tutor's Resource Pack has also been prepared to complement the Student's Book; this includes further tasks and support material for tutors.

RSA Examinations Board here records its thanks to the author, Veronica Cosier, and to the companies that allowed their experiences with information technology to be used in the book.

Martin Cross
Chief Executive
RSA Examinations Board

Introduction

THE SCHEME

Integrated Business Technology Stage II is an RSA scheme that provides opportunities for you to be assessed in four application areas using computers. The scheme consists of five assignments. The first four cover the applications: Databases, Spreadsheets, Word Processing and Graphical Representations. The fifth assignment involves integration of the files that you have created using the other four applications – Integrate Files and Present a Document. The scheme is designed for candidates who wish to extend their computer literacy and information technology skills using the type of integrated software packages found in a business environment.

The five Elements of Certification are:

1 SET UP AND USE THE FACILITIES OF A DATABASE STRUCTURE

2 CREATE AND USE A SPREADSHEET TO AID PROBLEM SOLVING

3 USE WORD PROCESSING FACILITIES TO PRODUCE A MULTI-PAGE DOCUMENT

4 PRODUCE GRAPHICAL REPRESENTATIONS OF NUMERIC DATA

5 INTEGRATE FILES AND PRESENT A DOCUMENT.

The scheme is designed to assess IT skills, but it also tests, through the use of source documentation, the candidate's ability to select relevant data from business documents.

Businesses operate in many different ways, from the choice of house style to the content and layout of their data. Therefore, a number of different layouts are used, particularly in the spreadsheet excercises, to reflect the differences that candidates are likely to meet when they join a company.

The File Store Record Sheet

The File Store Record Sheet has been introduced into the scheme to assist you in keeping a record of the work that you have completed. It is particularly useful when carrying out Element 5, Integrate Files and Present a Document, as you will require files which you stored when carrying out the other assignments.

You will find a copy of the File Store Record Sheet on page 96. You should use it when carrying out the assignments in this book. In each of the assignments you will be instructed several times to save files and record the details on the File Store Record Sheet. The main reason for the use of the sheet is to encourage the use of appropriate file management techniques and good business practice.

Retaining a copy of the File Store Record Sheet is important. If, for any reason your paper is lost, or some other query arises, then your tutor will be able to reprint your work.

It is recommended that the **files are not deleted until after your work has been certificated.**

THE BOOK

The book has been written primarily for RSA's Integrated Business Technology Stage II (IBTII) scheme, but it can be used by anyone who wants practice in the development of the use of the software applications, and also to develop file handling and management skills.

You may use this book with or without the help of a teacher or tutor. If you are working alone, you will need to refer to your computer software manual to find out the exact instructions for your software. The book cannot give you these instructions because of the many different programs available.

How to use this book

This book is set out in sections for each of the assignments:

- Databases
- Spreadsheets
- Word Processing
- Graphical Representations of Numeric Data
- Integrate Files and Present a Document.

Each of the applications can be used independently of the others and you can use them in any order. However, you will need to refer to the relevant source documentation to carry out the tasks and assignments. You will also need copies of the File Store Record Sheet to keep a note of your storage details in order to use the files again in the Integrate Files and Present a Document section.

In each application section you will find:

- build up exercises – these will introduce you to the requirements of the IBTII scheme within that application area
- a checklist – this is for you to complete to form a reference sheet
- a complete IBTII specimen assignment – this will provide assessment practice to help you monitor your progress.

All the build up tasks and specimen assignments have numbers printed down the right-hand side. These are the Assessment Objectives in RSA's Integrated Business Technology Scheme Stage II.

THE RSA INTEGRATED BUSINESS TECHNOLOGY STAGE II ASSESSMENT SCHEME

How will you be assessed?

You will be assessed in the practical use of the computer applications by completing assignments. These assignments are prepared by RSA. Assignments are written to cover the Assessment Objectives of the scheme. Full details of the scheme can be found in the RSA syllabus (see pages 92–95).

You are allowed 2 hours to complete each of the assignments. Printing may be done outside the time allowed for each assignment.

The IBTII scheme allows for assessment to be carried out at the Centre's discretion. Each candidate can attempt the assignment when he or she is ready to do so. This means that you may, for example, spend 6 weeks developing your spreadsheet skills and then undertake the assignment, or you may spend 6 months developing the skills and then attempt the assignment. If you do not achieve all the Assessment Objectives to be awarded the Element of Certification you may be permitted to have a second, completely new, attempt at the same assignment.

When you are ready for assessment your Centre will provide you with all the materials required. You may be presented with the materials for each assignment when you are ready to undertake assessment, or the Centre may go through the entire set of assignments with you, to give you the broader picture, before you begin assessment.

Presentation of the assessment materials is at the Centre's discretion. It is advisable to make enquiries about this before you begin assessment.

There is no time limit on the submission of work for certification.

Your work will be assessed locally (usually by the course tutor or lecturer) and then forwarded to an assigned RSA Marking Co-ordinator for external moderation.

How many applications are you required to do?

You may attempt any of the assignments and if you are successful in achieving all the Assessment Objectives and Performance Criteria for that assignment, then you will be awarded that particular Element of Certification. Because the final assignment, Integrate Files and Present a Document, is a combination of the other four assignments, you cannot undertake this assignment unless and until you have completed the other four.

How can you be successful?

The syllabus clearly identifies the Assessment Objectives and the Performance Criteria required to achieve those objectives. When completing the assignments you must demonstrate that you have achieved the Assessment Objectives.

Assessment Objectives	Performance Criteria
1.1 SELECT the relevant data	(a) Only required data is included
1.3 ENTER the data	(a) All data entered with no more than 3 Data Entry Errors
	(b) Data is encoded

You can see from the syllabus extract that in the database application you must **only include required data,** and that you are required to **enter the data** with no more than three data entry errors. If you include data that is not required, you will not be credited with 1.1. If you have more than three data entry errors you will not be credited with 1.3. In either case, this would prevent you from achieving the Element of Certification SET UP AND USE THE FACILITIES OF A DATABASE STRUCTURE.

Assessment Objectives relating to the entry of data must be carried out to the level of accuracy specified in the Performance Criteria. Assessment Objectives relating to the manipulation and alteration of data must be carried out with complete accuracy and must satisfy all the relevant Performance Criteria.

What certificate will you be awarded?

Certificates will be awarded as follows:

- Candidates who qualify for one or more Elements of Certification will be awarded an Integrated Business Technology Profile Certificate, listing all the Elements in which they have demonstrated competence.

- Candidates who meet the Assessment Objectives for all five Elements of Certification will be awarded a Stage II Pass Certificate in Integrated Business Technology, listing all the Elements of the scheme.

Re-entry and additions to certificates

If you **do not achieve** Element 5 INTEGRATE FILES AND PRESENT A DOCUMENT, you may only re-enter for a full set of assignments. You will be certificated for your achievement in the normal way. If you have been awarded a Profile Certificate **that includes** Element 5 and you wish to upgrade your certificate with additional Elements of Certification, you may re-enter for any of the Elements that you did not achieve. All additional Elements achieved will be added to the Profile Certificate. If this results in all five Elements of Certification being achieved, a full Stage II Pass Certificate will be issued.

Second attempts

Prior to your work being sent to the Marking Co-ordinator, you are allowed a second, completely fresh, attempt at the same assignment if you did not achieve all the Assessment Objectives at your first attempt.

Tutors may show the candidate the work, and discuss the reasons why the candidate did not achieve all the Assessment Objectives and Peformance Criteria. At this point, the tutor may want to allow the candidate to carry out further excercises, before attempting the assignment for the second time. The candidates may **not** use the printouts or files from the first attempt.

Only printouts from either the first or second attempt (not a combination of the two) may be used for assessment purposes.

THE ASSIGNMENTS

The assignments in chapters 1–5 are based on an interior design and supply company, Stallman Interiors. Stallman Interiors has a number of outlets around the country, and services customers throughout England and Wales. The company's Managing Director is Peter Stallman.

Peter has been at the forefront of introducing computers into the operation. The personal service that his customers have come to expect can only be delivered if he continues to develop the business. He believes that computer data allows him the benefit of substantial analysis and forecasting facilities previously too complex to compile.

The company uses the computer system to keep records of customers, suppliers and stock. Pat Ryan oversees the day-to-day transactions carried out around the country, whilst Peter uses the management information system for financial planning and analysis.

Customers can purchase goods from any of the retail outlets. However, many customers require assistance in selecting suitable materials, and guidance in calculating the required quantities.

When a customer requests help in assessing a quantity, a company representative will call at the customer's premises and carry out detailed measurements of the specified areas. All details taken on site are recorded using portable electronic devices. The data is downloaded on returning to the company (or can be electronically transferred).

When the data has been entered into the system, costings are added according to the customer choice of material. A quotation is generated automatically, detailing quantity, price and lead time.

You are to complete some of the work carried out by Peter and Pat.

For each of the applications there are build up exercises and a full practice assignment. In each case, the build up exercises are based on the curtain sector of the business, and the full practice assignments are based on the carpet sector. To prepare the final documents you will carry out the following sets of assignments.

SET 1

1	DATABASE	Set up a database of customer records in the north, south and central areas.
2	SPREADSHEET	Create a spreadsheet which displays carpet sales for the year 1994. You will display the sales by area and indicate which representative obtained the sales. You will add further details, and adjust the value for the average cost per square metre for the carpet range from the 1994 value to the 1995 value.
3	WORD PROCESSING	You will create a report (to a given specification) outlining business in Wales.
4	GRAPHICS	You will create a pie chart showing the number of customers by area (north, south and central) in 1994. You will also create a bar chart showing the value of sales for carpets installed in the north, south and central areas in 1994.
5	INTEGRATE FILES AND PRESENT A DOCUMENT	The fifth assignment involves the preparation of the final document. It will be prepared by amending your Word Processing file, and including extracts from the Database and Spreadsheet assignments and the pie chart from the Graphics assignment, where instructed.

SET 2

1	DATABASE	Set up a database of curtain supplier records.
2	SPREADSHEET	Create a spreadsheet which displays curtain sales for the year 1994. You should display both the supplier and which representative obtained the sales. You will add a column to display VAT, and adjust the value of the price per metre to project new values.
3	WORD PROCESSING	You will create a report (to a given specification) outlining some problems which have been experienced.
4	GRAPHICS	You will create a pie chart showing the number of customers provided with curtaining products in 1994 by each representative in Wales. You will also create a bar chart showing the value of curtain sales by supplier in Wales in 1994.
5	INTEGRATE FILES AND PRESENT A DOCUMENT	The fifth assignment involves the preparation of the final document. It will be prepared by amending your Word Processing file, and including extracts from the Database and Spreadsheet assignments and the bar chart from the Graphics assignment, where instructed.

Points for special attention

- The format required for the document in assignment 5 covers all sections of that report, i.e. you must apply the format to the sections extracted from the Database and Spreadsheet assignments.

- As the final document is a combination of the other assignments, it is advisable to use the same font/typeface for all the assignments. You may use any font/typeface that can be increased by two points. You MUST use the same font/typeface for assignments 3 and 5.

- Remember to save using a **unique** filename **each time**.

Databases

BUILD UP EXERCISES

1

TASK 1

What's this task for?

This task is designed to allow you to practise some of the skills required to gain IBTII assessment objectives

1.1	Select the relevant data
1.2	Enter the record structure
1.3	Enter the data
1.6	Create reports
1.7	Save data, structure, subsets and reports
1.8	Record file storage details
1.9	Print reports

Before you begin

You will need to find out and note down how to:

- select the relevant data
- enter the record structure
- enter the data
- create reports
- save data, structure, subsets and reports
- record file storage details
- print reports.

There is a checklist for you to complete on page 16 to use as a reference sheet.

OBJECTIVES

1 Using the information on the **DATA SHEETS** (pages 56–68), set up a database of curtain supplier records. Ensure that the field width is adjusted to accommodate the data. You must use the following field headings in your reports (a guide is given to the field content).

1.2(a) (c)

1.2(b)

HEADING	FIELD CONTENT
SUPNAME	SUPPLIER
SUPLOC	SUPPLIER LOCATION
REP	REPRESENTATIVE
CUSTCON	CUSTOMER NAME
AREA	AREA, i.e. WALES, NORTH, SOUTH or CENTRAL
TCODE	TRANSPORT using the following codes:
	CODE TRANSPORT
	C CARRIER
	S 24 HOURS
	V VAN
DATE	INSTALLATION DATE

2 Enter the relevant data. You should include **ONLY** the details shown for **CURTAIN SUPPLIERS**. **Note**: If you include other information you will be penalised (i.e. you will not achieve 1.1(a)).

1.1(a)
1.3(a) (b)

OBJECTIVES

3 Save the data using a unique filename, and record the details on the File Store Record Sheet.

1.7(a) (d)
1.8(a)

4 Create a report in table format to display **ALL** the records. Use the headings given above. Save the report using a unique filename, and record the details on the File Store Record Sheet.

1.6(a) (d)
1.7(c) (d)
1.8(a)

5 Print the report in table format, including the field headings.

1.9(a) (b) (c)

BUILD UP EXERCISES

TASK 2

What's this task for?

This task is designed to allow you to practise some of the skills required to gain IBTII assessment objectives.

1.5	Sort data (alphanumeric/numeric)
1.6	Create reports
1.7	Save data, structure, subsets and reports
1.8	Record file storage details
1.9	Print reports

Before you begin

You will need to find out and note down how to:

■ sort data (alphanumeric/numeric).

There is a checklist for you to complete on page 16 to use as a reference sheet.

OBJECTIVES

1 Reload the database file saved in Task 1.

2 Sort the list into **ASCENDING DATE** order.   **1.5(a)**

3 Save the list, using a unique filename, in **ASCENDING DATE** order. Record the details on the File Store Record Sheet.   **1.7(a)** **1.8(a)**

4 Create a report in table format, include the field headings, and display the following fields **ONLY**:   **1.6(a) (b)**

REP ■ CUSTCON ■ AREA ■ TCODE ■ DATE

5 Save the report using a unique filename, and record the details on the File Store Record Sheet.   **1.7(c) (d)** **1.8(a)**

6 Print the report in table format, including the field headings.   **1.9(a) (b) (c)**

TASK 3

What's this task for?

This task is designed to allow you to practise some of the skills required to gain IBTII assessment objectives

1.4	**Search on three criteria to select a subset of the data**
1.6	**Create reports**
1.7	**Save data, structure, subsets and reports**
1.8	**Record file storage details**
1.9	**Print reports**

Before you begin

You will need to find out and note down how to:

■ search on three criteria to select a subset of the data.

There is a checklist for you to complete on page 16 to use as a reference sheet.

OBJECTIVES

1 Reload the database file saved in Task 2.

2 Search for those customers in **WALES** who had **CURTAINS INSTALLED** in **1994** – the delivery should have been by **VAN**. Save the list using a unique filename, and record the details on the File Store Record Sheet.

        1.4(a)
        1.7(b) (d)
        1.8(a)

3 Using the search list from 2 above, create a report in table format to display **ONLY** the fields indicated below, in the order shown:

SUPNAME ■ **SUPLOC** ■ **CUSTCON** ■ **REP**

        1.6(c) (d)

4 Save the report using a unique filename, and record the details on the File Store Record Sheet.

        1.7(c) (d)
        1.8(a)

5 Print the report in table format, including the field headings.

        1.9(a) (b) (c)

DATABASE CHECKLIST

You should complete this checklist for each hardware and software combination you use. Use information from your tutor, handouts, handbooks and software manuals to complete the list. You can then use your list as a reference sheet to complete the practice task that follows.

IBTII REF	ASSESSMENT OBJECTIVE	HOW TO DO IT
1.2	Enter the record structure	
1.3	Enter the data	
1.4	Search on three criteria to select a subset of the data	
1.5	Sort data (alphanumeric/numeric)	
1.6	Create reports	
1.7	Save data, structure, subsets and reports	
1.8	Record file storage details	
1.9	Print reports	

TASK 4

What's this task for?

This task is designed to allow you to practise a complete assignment.
It covers all the IBTII Database assessment objectives. You **cannot**
use this assignment for assessment purposes.

OBJECTIVES

1 Using the information on the **DATA SHEETS** (pages 56–68), set up a database
of customer records. Ensure that the field width is adjusted to accommodate
the data. You must use the following field headings in your reports
(a guide is given to the field content).

1.2(a) (c)

1.2(b)

HEADING	FIELD CONTENT
NAME	CUSTOMER NAME (Surname only)
CODE	AREA CODE
NO	TELEPHONE NO (do not include code here)
COMPANY	COMPANY
TOWN	TOWN
AREA	NORTH, SOUTH or CENTRAL
PC	PRODUCT CATEGORY using the following codes:
	P CARPET
	T CURTAINING
INSTALLED	INSTALLATION DATE

FULL PRACTICE ASSIGNMENT

		OBJECTIVES
2	Enter the relevant data. You should include **ONLY** the details shown for the **NORTH**, **SOUTH** and **CENTRAL** areas.	**1.1(a)** **1.3(a) (b)**
3	Save the data using a unique filename, and record the details on the File Store Record Sheet.	**1.7(a) (d)** **1.8(a)**
4	Create a report in table format to display **ALL** the records. Use the headings given above. Save the report using a unique filename, and record the details on the File Store Record Sheet.	**1.6(a) (d)** **1.7(c) (d)** **1.8(a)**
5	Print the report in table format, including the field headings.	**1.9(a) (b) (c)**
6	Sort the list into **ASCENDING** order of **INSTALLATION DATE**.	**1.5(a)**
7	Save the list, using a unique filename, in **ASCENDING** order of **INSTALLED DATE**. Record the details on the File Store Record Sheet.	**1.7(a) (d)** **1.8(a)**

FULL PRACTICE ASSIGNMENT

	OBJECTIVES

8 Create a report in table format, include the field headings, and display the following fields **ONLY**:

NAME ■ **TOWN** ■ **INSTALLED**

1.6(b) (d)

---

9 Save the report using a unique filename, and record the details on the File Store Record Sheet.

1.7(c) (d)
1.8(a)

---

10 Print the report in table format, including the field headings.

1.9(a) (b) (c)

---

11 Search for those customers in the **SOUTH** who had **CARPET INSTALLED in 1994**. Save the list using a unique filename, and record the details on the File Store Record Sheet.

1.4(a)
1.7(b) (d)
1.8(a)

---

12 Using the search list from 11, create a report in table format to display **ONLY** the fields indicated below, in the order shown:

NAME ■ **TOWN** ■ **COMPANY**

1.6(c) (d)

---

13 Save the report using a unique filename, and record the details on the File Store Record Sheet.

1.7(c) (d)
1.8(a)

---

14 Print the report in table format, including the field headings.

1.9(a) (b) (c)

Spreadsheets

TASK 1

What's this task for?

This task is designed to allow you to practise some of the skills required to gain IBTII assessment objectives

2.1	Select the relevant data
2.2	Enter the spreadsheet layout
2.3	Enter text and data into the spreadsheet
2.4	Generate and apply formulae
2.7	Save structure and data
2.8	Record file storage details
2.9	Print the spreadsheet data

Before you begin

You will need to find out and note down how to:
- select the relevant data
- enter the spreadsheet layout
- enter text and data into the spreadsheet
- generate and apply formulae
- save structure and data
- record file storage details
- print the spreadsheet data.

There is a checklist for you to complete on page 24 to use as a reference sheet.

OBJECTIVES

Create a spreadsheet which displays sales of each type of curtain for the year **1994**. You should display only the sales in **Wales**, and indicate both the supplier and the representative who obtained the sale. Display the supplier codes, and the number of metres sold under the curtain codes.

1 Enter the title: **SUPPLIER SALES 1994 – WALES**   2.3(a)

Your spreadsheet must include:

SUPPLIER	REPRESENTATIVE	CC9	CS10	AC11	AS12	PC13	PS14	COST/M 1994	VALUE	SUPPLIER CODE	SUPPLIER TOTAL
TOTALS											

OBJECTIVES

NOTE
When you enter the data for this task, you will find that only a limited number of cells are used under the product codes.

Remember that even if no data is entered in cells, they can still be included in a formula range. Indeed, it can be useful to do so, because at a later date if you do enter data into any of the cells, you will not have to amend the corresponding formula.

2 Using the information on the **DATA SHEETS** (pages 56–68) and the **MATERIAL COSTS SHEET** (page 69), enter the text and numeric data for the quantities of **CURTAIN SALES** in **1994** for **WALES**. Where there is more than one entry for a supplier (e.g. Abbot) ensure that the data is grouped together. Ensure that the text is left aligned, that column headings are right aligned, that figures are right aligned and that any monetary amounts are displayed to 2 decimal places.	**2.1(a)** **2.2(a) (b) (c)** **(d) (e) (f)** **2.3(a) (b)**
3 Using the appropriate formula, generate a total in the **VALUE** column **(TOTAL OF PRODUCT CODE ITEMS × COST/M 1994)** for the first supplier. Replicate this formula for each of the other suppliers.	**2.4(a) (b)**
4 Using the appropriate formula, generate a total in the **SUPPLIER TOTAL** column for each of the suppliers.	**2.4(a)**
5 On the **TOTALS** row, using the appropriate formula, generate a total for product code **CC9**. Replicate this formula for each of the other product codes.	**2.4(a) (b)**
6 On the **TOTALS** row, using the appropriate formula, generate a total in the **VALUE** column.	**2.4(a)**
7 Save the spreadsheet using a unique filename, and enter the filename on the File Store Record Sheet. Print the spreadsheet.	**2.7(a) (b) (c)** **2.8(a)** **2.9(a) (b) (c)**

BUILD UP EXERCISES

TASK 2

What's this task for?

This task is designed to allow you to practise some of the skills required to gain IBTII assessment objectives

2.5	Insert a column/row
2.6	Generate projections
2.7	Save structure and data
2.8	Record file storage details
2.9	Print the spreadsheet data

Before you begin

You will need to find out and note down how to:

■ insert a column/row

■ generate projections.

There is a checklist for you to complete on page 24 to use as a reference sheet.

OBJECTIVES

1 Reload the spreadsheet file saved in Task 1.

---

2 Insert a column headed **VAT**, after the column headed **VALUE** and before the column headed **SUPPLIER CODE**. Use the appropriate formula to generate the amount (17.5% of VALUE) for the first supplier. Replicate this formula for each of the other suppliers.   2.4(a) (b)   2.5(a) (b)

On the **TOTAL** row, use the appropriate formula to generate a total for the **VAT** column you have just inserted. Ensure that the column heading is right aligned, that figures are right aligned and that monetary amounts are displayed to 2 decimal places.   2.4(a)   2.2(b) (c) (e) (f)

---

3 Save the spreadsheet using a unique filename, and enter the filename on the File Store Record Sheet. Print the spreadsheet.   2.7(a) (b) (c)   2.8(a)   2.9(a) (b) (c)

---

4 Print the data in the **SUPPLIER CODE** and **SUPPLIER TOTAL** columns **ONLY.**   2.7(d)   2.9(a) (c)

---

5 Change the cost per metre **(COST/M)** for **ALL** the **PRODUCT CODES** to £9.45.   2.6(a)

---

6 Alter the heading of the column to **COST/M AV 95.**   2.6(b)

---

7 Save your file using a unique filename, and record the details on the File Store Record Sheet.   2.7(a) (b) (c)   2.8(a)

---

8 Print the spreadsheet.   2.9(a) (b) (c)

TASK 3

What's this task for?

This task is designed to allow you to practise some of the skills required to gain IBTII assessment objectives

2.7	Save structure and data
2.8	Record file storage details
2.10	Print spreadsheet formulae

Before you begin

You will need to find out and note down how to:

- print spreadsheet formulae.

There is a checklist for you to complete on page 24 to use as a reference sheet.

OBJECTIVES

1 Reload the spreadsheet file saved in Task 2.

2 Print the spreadsheet **FORMULAE** in the **VALUE** and **VAT** columns. Ensure that you print the formulae **in full**.

2.10(a)

SPREADSHEET CHECKLIST

You should complete this checklist for each hardware and software combination you use. Use information from your tutor, handouts, handbooks and software manuals to complete the list. You can then use your list as a reference sheet to complete the practice task that follows.

IBTII REF	ASSESSMENT OBJECTIVE	HOW TO DO IT
2.2	Enter the spreadsheet layout	
2.3	Enter text and data into the spreadsheet	
2.4	Generate and apply formulae	
2.5	Insert a column/row	
2.6	Generate projections	
2.7	Save structure and data	
2.8	Record file storage details	
2.9	Print the spreadsheet data	
2.10	Print spreadsheet formulae	

FULL PRACTICE ASSIGNMENT

TASK 4

What's this task for?

This task is designed to allow you to practise a complete assignment. It covers all the IBTII Spreadsheet assessment objectives. You **cannot** use this assignment for assessment purposes.

OBJECTIVES

Create a spreadsheet which displays **carpet sales** for the year **1994**. You should display the sales by area and indicate which representative obtained the sales. Display the square metres of carpet for each code.

1 Enter the title: **CARPET SALES 1994**   2.3(a)
   Your spreadsheet must include:

AREA	REP	SALES TOTAL	AREA TOTAL	AV SQ M 1994	TOTAL NO	SHBI	SRB2	STHB3	STRB4	CE5
NORTH										
SOUTH										
CENTRAL										
OVERALL TOTALS										

NOTE
You can see from the spreadsheet layout above that the total for the product codes is placed to the left of the data entries which contribute to the total.

This may be the preferred choice, because, when viewing on screen, you would have all the 'total' data showing rather than the detail. This would be one way to avoid having to switch between screens to view data. As a result of this placing, the other formulae dependent on the result are also placed to the left.

FULL PRACTICE ASSIGNMENT

2 Using the information on the **DATA SHEETS** (pages 56–68) and the **MATERIAL COSTS SHEET** (page 69), enter the text and numeric data for the quantities of carpet sales in 1994 for the **NORTH, SOUTH** and **CENTRAL** areas. Do not include the item T6 Tiles. Use the average cost per square metre for the year.

Ensure that the text and column headings are left aligned. All figures must be right aligned. The product code quantity figures should be displayed in integer format. All monetary amounts should be displayed to 2 decimal places. Cell widths must be set to display all data in full.

2.1(a)
2.2(a) (b) (c)
(d) (e) (f)
2.3(a) (b)

3 Using the appropriate formula, generate a total (of product code entries) in the **TOTAL NO** column for the first representative. Replicate this formula for each of the other representatives.

2.4 (a) (b)

4 Using the appropriate formula, generate a total in the **SALES TOTAL** column for the first representative (AV SQ M 1994 x TOTAL NO). Replicate this formula for each of the other representatives.

2.4 (a) (b)

5 Using the appropriate formulae, generate a total in the **AREA TOTAL** column for sales in each of the **NORTH, SOUTH** and **CENTRAL** areas.

2.4 (a)

6 On the **OVERALL TOTALS** row, using the appropriate formula, generate a total for product code **SHB1**. Replicate this formula for each of the other product codes.

2.4 (a) (b)

7 On the **OVERALL TOTALS** row, using the appropriate formula, generate a total for the **AREA TOTAL** column.

2.4 (a)

8 Save the spreadsheet using a unique filename, and enter the filename on the File Store Record Sheet.

2.7 (a) (b) (c)
2.8 (a)

9 Print the spreadsheet.

2.9 (a) (b) (c)

10 It has been decided to include the sales for the product **T6 TILES**. Using the information on the **DATA SHEETS**, enter the data for this product. Insert the column, headed **T6**, after the column headed **TOTAL NO** and before the column headed **SHB1**. Ensure that the data in this added column is included in the formulae in the **TOTAL NO** column.

2.1(a)
2.3(a) (b)
2.5(a) (b)

On the **OVERALL TOTALS** row, use the appropriate formula to generate a total for the **T6** column you have just inserted. Ensure that the column heading is left aligned.

2.2(b) (c)
2.4(a)

FULL PRACTICE ASSIGNMENT

	OBJECTIVES

11 Save the spreadsheet using a unique filename, and enter the filename on the File Store Record Sheet. Print the spreadsheet.

2.7(a) (b) (c)
2.8(a)
2.9(a) (b) (c)

---

12 Print the columns headed **AREA, REP, SALES TOTAL** and **AREA TOTAL**. Include the spreadsheet title.

2.7(d)
2.9(a) (c)

---

13 Print the spreadsheet **formulae** in the **SALES TOTAL** and **AREA TOTAL** columns. Ensure that you print the formulae **in full**.

2.10(a)

---

14 Using the information on the **MATERIAL COSTS SHEET** (page 69) change the figure for the average cost per square metre for the carpet range from the 1994 value to the 1995 value. Amend the **AV SQ M 1994** text to reflect this change.

2.6(a) (b)

---

15 Save your file using a unique filename, and record the details on the File Store Record Sheet.

2.7(a) (b) (c)
2.8(a)

---

16 Print the spreadsheet.

2.9(a) (b) (c)

Word processing **3**

BUILD UP EXERCISES

TASK 1

What's this task for?

This task is designed to allow you to practise some of the skills required to gain IBTII assessment objectives

3.1	**Implement a document format**
	Set top margin
	Set left margin
	Set line length
	Set line spacing
	Set justification ON/OFF
	Set character size
3.2	**Enter the data**
3.4	**Use indentation**
3.8	**Save the document**
3.9	**Record file storage details**
3.10	**Print the document**

Before you begin

You will need to find out and note down how to:

- implement a document format
  set top margin
  set left margin
  set line length
  set line spacing
  set justification ON/OFF
  set character size
- enter the data
- use indentation
- save the document
- record file storage details
- print the document.

There is a checklist for you to complete on page 34 to use as a reference sheet.

OBJECTIVES

1 Create a file to the specification shown below.

Top margin	Not less than 1.3 cm ($\frac{1}{2}$")	**3.1(a)**
Left margin	Not less than 1.3 cm ($\frac{1}{2}$")	**3.1(b)**
Line length	16.5 cm (6 $\frac{1}{2}$")	**3.1(c)**
Line spacing	Single	**3.1(d)**
Alignment	Left aligned, ragged right margin	**3.1(e)**
Character size	12 point or 12 cpi	**3.1(f)**
Paper size	A4	**3.10(a)**

2 Enter the following text. Save the file using a unique filename, and record the details on the File Store Record Sheet. Print one copy of the file on A4 paper.

    3.2(a)
    3.8(a) (b)
    3.9(a)
    3.10(a) (b) (c)

MATERIAL SUITABILITY

There is a variety of tests that can be performed in order to find out if a material is suitable for production.

1   Key Tear

      This test is used to determine whether or not perforations are likely to tear during lasting operations or wear. It is also an aid in deciding the best size of hole punch.

2   Lasting Area

      This test shows how much strain the upper can undergo whilst being lasted over a very pointed toe shaped last, before it will rip, and then tear.

3   Martendale Abrasion

      This test will show how much abrasion the material coating can withstand before the surface is worn.

4   Chemical

      Chemical tests will tell us which treatment the leather has undergone in the finishing process.

5   Flexometer

      This test ascertains how much wear the soling material can withstand before it begins to crack under the strain of wear.

BUILD UP EXERCISES

TASK 2

What's this task for?

This task is designed to allow you to practise some of the
skills required to gain IBTII assessment objectives

3.1 **Implement a document format**
  Set top margin
  Set left margin
  Set line length
  Set line spacing
  Set justification ON/OFF
  Set character size

3.2 **Enter the data**

3.4 **Use indentation**

3.6 **Present a table**

3.8 **Save the document**

3.9 **Record file storage details**

3.10 **Print the document**

Before you begin

You will need to find out and note down how to:

■ present a table.

There is a checklist for you to complete on page 34 to use as a reference sheet.

		OBJECTIVES
1 Create a file to the specification shown below.		
Top margin	Not less than 1.3 cm ($\frac{1}{2}$ ")	3.1(a)
Left margin	Not less than 1.3 cm ($\frac{1}{2}$ ")	3.1(b)
Line length	16.5 cm (6 $\frac{1}{2}$ ")	3.1(c)
Line spacing	Double	3.1(d)
Alignment	Left aligned, ragged right margin	3.1(e)
Character size	12 point or 12 cpi	3.1(f)
Paper size	A4	3.10(a)

2 Enter the text below. Save the file using a unique filename, and
record the details on the File Store Record Sheet. Print one copy
of the file on A4 paper.

3.2(a)
3.8(a) (b)
3.9(a)
3.10(a) (b) (c)

Carwen Products Welsh Sector Report

Last year Carwen Products continued to offer specialist products to every sector of the market. However, the largest proportion of our sales is to the retail sector.

Market share remains higher than that of our closest competitors (details below).

COMPANY	LOCATION
Salisbury Sales	Cardiff
Ingres Interiors	Bristol
Trend Setters	Birmingham
Petra Fabrics	Leeds

SALESFORCE

Our salesforce offers years of experience, product and market knowledge, and continues to develop business.

It possesses the latest details regarding service information. Many staff have increased sales with their key accounts.

TRANSPORT

Our decision to introduce company vans has provided increased benefits. We now provide a local delivery service twice weekly, with many areas served three times weekly. Deliveries are supported by carrier services, and a 24 hour delivery service. The following customers have expressed their satisfaction with this new service:

BRANCH NETWORK

Our network continues to thrive. Carwen Products have developed an experienced, knowledgeable staff throughout the country to provide a local, direct service, a product range second to none, and vast stockholding.

BUILD UP EXERCISES

STOCKHOLDING AND PRODUCT RANGE

We hold an extensive product range across our branches, at generous levels, to satisfy local needs immediately.

We have been working on a collection of accessories, and the following items will be added to our catalogue which will be circulated next month.

1   CURTAIN POLES

A premier collection of made-to-measure curtain poles in polished and lacquered solid brass, natural, stained and painted wood.

2   TRIMMINGS COLLECTION

This collection includes curtain tiebacks (in reels or cut to length service). We offer 18 rich colourways and 11 trim options.

3   CURTAIN ACCESSORIES AND PRE-PACKAGED POLES

We offer a range of decorative curtain accessories - solid brass tassel hooks and holdbacks, holdbacks in marble and ceramics, a colourful range of tassel tiebacks, and solid brass coronas. We also include a range of wood and brass curtain poles.

SUPPLIER RELATIONSHIPS

Please note the graph for supplier sales in 1994.

We continue to develop excellent working relationships with our suppliers. The sales figures below show the values from the graph of supplier sales (1994).

TASK 3

What's this task for?

This task is designed to allow you to practise some of the skills required to gain IBTII assessment objectives

3.1	**Implement a document format**
	Set top margin
	Set left margin
	Insert a page break
3.3	**Use emphasis**
3.5	**Centre line(s)**
3.7	**Number the pages**
3.8	**Save the document**
3.9	**Record file storage details**
3.10	**Print the document**

Before you begin

You will need to find out and note down how to:

- implement a document format
  insert a page break
- use emphasis
- centre line(s)
- number the pages.

There is a checklist for you to complete on page 34 to use as a reference sheet.

OBJECTIVES

1 Reload the word processing file saved in Task 2.

---

2 CENTRE and EMPHASISE the heading: **3.3(a)**
   Carwen Products Welsh Sector Report **3.5(a)**

---

3 Number the pages: **Bottom centre. Start at 8.** **3.7(a) (b)**

---

4 Insert page breaks as follows: **3.1(g)**
   (i) before the **TRANSPORT** paragraph
   (ii) in the **STOCKHOLDING AND PRODUCT RANGE** section before
       We have been working on a collection...

---

5 Restrict the document to 3 pages. You may need to adjust the margins **3.1(a)**
   to accommodate this. Retain the line length of 16.5 cm ($6\frac{1}{2}$").

---

6 Save the file using a unique filename, and record the details on the **3.8(a) (b)**
   File Store Record Sheet. **3.9(a)**

---

7 Print one copy of the file on A4 paper. **3.10(a) (b) (c)**

WORD PROCESSING CHECKLIST

You should complete this checklist for each hardware and software combination you use. Use information from your tutor, handouts, handbooks and software manuals to complete the list. You can then use your list as a reference sheet to complete the practice task that follows.

IBTII REF	ASSESSMENT OBJECTIVE	HOW TO DO IT
3.1	Implement a document format	
	Set top margin	
	Set left margin	
	Set line length	
	Set line spacing	
	Set justification ON/OFF	
	Set character size	
	Insert a page break	
3.2	Enter the data	
3.3	Use emphasis	
3.4	Use indentation	
3.5	Centre line(s)	
3.6	Present a table	
3.7	Number the pages	
3.8	Save the document	
3.9	Record file storage details	
3.10	Print the document	

FULL PRACTICE ASSIGNMENT

TASK 4

What's this task for?

This task is designed to allow you to practise a complete assignment.
It covers all the IBTII Word Processing assessment objectives.
You **cannot** use this assignment for assessment purposes.

OBJECTIVES

1 Create a file to the specification shown below. You may use any
font/typeface that can be increased by 2 points. When carrying out
the assignments for assessment, you **MUST** use the same font/typeface
for assignment 5, Integrate Files and Present a Document.

Top margin	Not less than 1.3 cm ($\frac{1}{2}$ ")	3.1(a)
Left margin	Not less than 1.3 cm ($\frac{1}{2}$ ")	3.1(b)
Line length	14 cm (5 $\frac{1}{2}$ ")	3.1(c)
Line spacing	Single	3.1(d)
Alignment	Justified	3.1(e)
Character size	14 point or 10 cpi	3.1(f)
Paper size	A4	3.10(a)
Page numbers	Bottom left. Start at 1	3.7(a) (b)

2 Enter the text below. Save the file using a unique filename, and
record the details on the File Store Record Sheet. Print one copy
of the file on A4 paper.

3.2(a)
3.8(a) (b)
3.9(a)
3.10(a) (b) (c)
3.5(a)

CUSTOMER CARE CENTRE ENQUIRY — centre

In the last year we have received a number
of complaints regarding our products. The
majority have been from our southern area.

This is of considerable concern as the south
is the highest yield area. I have provided
a profile of sales for your information.

The chart is a useful guide, but I also
include data below which gives you a
breakdown of the sales figures. Your
representatives —

FULL PRACTICE ASSIGNMENT

OBJECTIVES
3.4(a)

Wade
Weston
Davis
Cole
Hill
Winter

[Indent this section 38 mm (1½") from the left margin]

have performed extremely well, but we have received too many complaints.

I would be grateful if you would provide me with an analysis of these problems. Are there any areas of similarity? Was the product provided by any one supplier?

NEW PRODUCT DEVELOPMENT [emphasise] 3.3(a)

I have attached the text for our new advertising leaflet. Please discuss it with your representatives, and return any comments by the end of the week.

The chart below gives a breakdown of customers by area.

I believe we should use the following customers to provide the first series of outlets for the new flooring:

NEW PAGE

3.1(g)

Larin Duro from Katell is the next generation of flooring for the home.

A highly resilient surface, perfectly balanced by a classical printed base design - the result is an outstanding, multi-dimensional effect. It has a wonderfully hard wearing, easy to clean surface.

Larin Duro allows you to obtain a seamless finish in virtually every room. We are happy to accommodate customised orders. The standard range of colourways and widths follows:

COLOUR	WIDTH (METRES)
SILVER SHIMMER	4.75
LIVELY LAVENDER	4.5
BRONZED EARTH	4.25
FREE FOREST	4
MOONSTONE FIRE	3.75
CHILLED CHERRY	3.5

3.6(a)

Ensure that your next flooring has our quality certification. Up to now a dried-in stain on flooring was something you had to live with. With this new concept you can have stain resistance never achieved before.

Larin Duro has anti-static control that will last the life of the flooring, which means no more startling shocks, ever!

This is a completely new way of looking at flooring - take a look for yourself. Call 01552 2569933 for details of your nearest stockist.

Graphical representations of numeric data

4

░░

BUILD UP EXERCISES

TASK 1

What's this task for?

This task is designed to allow you to practise some of the skills required to gain IBTII assessment objectives

4.1	Select relevant data

4.2	Enter textheading on pie chart sector labels on pie chart OR legend on pie chart

4.3	Produce graphical representations of numeric data

4.4	Save the graphical representations

4.5	Record file storage details

4.6	Print the graphical representation

Before you begin

You will need to find out and note down how to:

- select relevant data
- enter text
  heading on pie chart
  sector labels on pie chart OR legend on pie chart
- produce graphical representations of numeric data
- save the graphical representation
- record file storage details
- print the graphical representation in portrait.

There is a checklist for you to complete on page 40 to use as a reference sheet.

OBJECTIVES

You will create a pie chart showing the number of customers provided with curtaining products in 1994 by each representative in Wales.

---

1 Using the information on the **DATA SHEETS** (pages 56–68), create a pie chart to show the curtain sales of each representative in Wales in 1994. Graph the sales by the number of customers.

4.1(a)
4.2(a)
4.3(a)

---

2 The chart must be titled: **REPRESENTATIVE ACCOUNTS**

4.2(e)

---

3 The sectors must be labelled with the representative's name **(WILLIAMSON, BOSTON** and **HARDCASTLE)**, or a legend should be attached to identify the sections. A numeric value or a percentage division should also be shown.

4.2(f)
4.3(c)

---

4 Save the display using a unique filename, and enter the filename on the File Store Record Sheet.

4.4(a) (b) (c)
4.5(a)

---

5 Print the graphical representation in portrait display.

4.6(a) (c)

TASK 2

What's this task for?

This task is designed to allow you to practise some of the skills required to gain IBTII assessment objectives

| 4.1 | Select relevant data |

| 4.2 | Enter text |
heading on bar chart
axes labels on bar chart
bar (variable) labels on bar chart

| 4.3 | Produce graphical representations of numeric data |

| 4.4 | Save the graphical representations |

| 4.5 | Record file storage details |

| 4.6 | Print the graphical representation |

Before you begin

You will need to find out and note down how to:

- select relevant data
- enter text
  heading on bar chart
  axes labels on bar chart
  bar (variable) labels on bar chart
- produce graphical representations of numeric data
- save the graphical representations
- record file storage details
- print the graphical representation in landscape.

There is a checklist for you to complete on page 40 to use as a reference sheet.

OBJECTIVES

You will prepare a bar chart showing the value of supplier sales for curtains provided in Wales in 1994.

---

1 Using the information on the **DATA SHEETS** (pages 56–68) and **MATERIAL COSTS SHEET** (page 69), create a bar chart to show the value of **CURTAIN SALES** by **SUPPLIER** in **WALES** in **1994**.
 4.1(a)
 4.2(a)
 4.3(a)

 Use the data for those curtain products **installed in 1994**, and graph the sales by supplier value. Use the supplier codes.

---

2 The chart must be titled: **SUPPLIER VALUE 1994**   4.2(b)

---

3 The X axis must be labelled: **SUPPLIER CODE**   4.2(c)

---

4 The Y axis must be labelled: **VALUE £**   4.2(c)

---

5 The Y axis scale must be: MIN: **0**   4.3(b)
                              MAX: **15,000**

---

6 The bars (variables) must be labelled with the **SUPPLIER CODE**.   4.2(d)

---

7 Save the display using a unique filename, and enter the filename on the File Store Record Sheet.   4.4(a) (b) (c)
                                                                                                       4.5(a)

---

8 Print the graphical representation in landscape display.   4.6(b) (c)

GRAPHICAL REPRESENTATION CHECKLIST

You should complete this checklist for each hardware and software combination you use. Use information from your tutor, handouts, handbooks and software manuals to complete the list. You can then use your list as a reference sheet to complete the practice task that follows.

IBTII REF	ASSESSMENT OBJECTIVE	HOW TO DO IT
4.2	Enter text	_____
	heading on bar chart	_____
	axes labels on bar chart	_____
	bar (variable) labels on bar chart	_____
	heading on pie chart	_____
	sector labels on pie chart OR legend on pie chart	_____
4.3	Produce graphical representations of numeric data	_____
	adjust scale on bar chart	_____
	display percentage or numeric value on pie chart segments	_____
4.4	Save the graphical representations	_____
4.5	Record file storage details	_____
4.6	Print the graphical representations	_____
	in portrait	_____
	in landscape	_____

TASK 3

What's this task for?

This task is designed to allow you to practise a complete assignment.
It covers all the IBTII Graphical Representation assessment objectives.
You **cannot** use this assignment for assessment purposes.

OBJECTIVES

You will create a pie chart showing the number of customers in the north,
south and central areas in 1994. You will also prepare a bar chart showing
the value of sales for carpets fitted in the north, south and central areas in 1994.

		OBJECTIVES
1	Using the information on the **DATA SHEETS** (pages 56–68), create a pie chart to show the number of customers in 1994, by area. You should use **ONLY** the data for the **NORTH, SOUTH** and **CENTRAL** areas. Graph the sales by the number of customers.	4.1(a) 4.2(a) 4.3(a)
2	The chart must be titled: **CUSTOMERS BY AREA**	4.2(e)
3	The sectors must be labelled with the area **(NORTH, SOUTH** and **CENTRAL)**, or a legend should be attached to identify the sections. A numeric value or a percentage division should also be shown.	4.2(f) 4.3(c)
4	Save the display using a unique filename, and enter the filename on the File Store Record Sheet.	4.4(a) (b) (c) 4.5(a)
5	Print the graphical representation in portrait display.	4.6(a) (c)
6	Using the information on the **DATA SHEETS** (pages 56–68) and **MATERIAL COSTS SHEET** (page 69), create a bar chart to show the value of **CARPET SALES.** Use the data for those carpets **fitted in 1994**, and graph the sales by area **(NORTH, SOUTH** and **CENTRAL)**.	4.1(a) 4.2(a) 4.3(a)
7	The chart must be titled: **SALES BY AREA**	4.2(b)
8	The X axis must be labelled: **AREA**	4.2(c)
9	The Y axis must be labelled: **AMOUNT £**	4.2(c)
10	The Y axis scale must be: MIN:**0** MAX: **300,000**	4.3(b)
11	The bars (variables) must be labelled with the area **(NORTH, SOUTH** and **CENTRAL)**, or suitable abbreviations.	4.2(d)
12	Save the display using a unique filename, and enter the filename on the File Store Record Sheet.	4.4(a) (b) (c) 4.5(a)
13	Print the graphical representation in landscape display.	4.6(b) (c)

Integrate files and present a document

5

BUILD UP EXERCISES

TASK 1

What's this task for?

This task is designed to allow you to practise some of the skills required to gain IBTII assessment objectives

5.1 Retrieve previously stored document

5.2 Import information from
database
spreadsheet
pie chart

5.4 Format information
set top margin
set left margin
set line length
set line spacing
set justification ON/OFF
control page numbers
position page numbers
set character size
re-size graphical representation
insert page breaks
repaginate

5.5 Save file

5.7 Record file storage details

5.8 Print document

Before you begin

You will need to find out and note down how to:

- retrieve previously stored document
- import information from
database
spreadsheet
pie chart
- format information
set top margin
set left margin
set line length
set line spacing
set justification ON/OFF
control page numbers
position page numbers
set character size
re-size graphical representation
insert page breaks
repaginate
- save file
- record file storage details
- print document.

There is a checklist for you to complete on page 51 to use as a reference sheet.

BUILD UP EXERCISES

Use the details on your File Store Record Sheet(s) to recall the following files:

APPLICATION	TASK	PRINT
Word Processing	3	1
Database	3	1
Spreadsheet	2	2
Graphics (PIE CHART)	1	1

You will see how they are to be used on pages 44–46.
Please ensure that the format specification covers the Database and Spreadsheet extracts of your document. The graphical representation must be legible and displayed within the margins.

---

1 Recall your Word Processing file and use the specification below to produce the final document. **5.1(a)**

Top margin	Not less than 1.3 cm ($\frac{1}{2}$")	**5.4(a)**
Left margin	Not less than 1.3 cm ($\frac{1}{2}$")	**5.4(b)**
Line length	15.3 cm (6")	**5.4(c)**
Line spacing	Single (except where indicated)	**5.4(d)**
Alignment	Justified	**5.4(e)**
Character size	10 point or 14 cpi (decrease size)	**5.4(h)**
Paper size	A4	**5.8(d)**
Paper numbers	Bottom left. Start at page 1.	**5.4(f) (g)**

---

2 If necessary, resize the pie chart and repaginate. Save the file using a unique filename, and record the details on the File Store Record Sheet. **5.4(i) (j) (l)**
5.5(a) (b)
5.7(a)

---

3 Print the document on A4 paper. **5.8(a) (b) (c)**
(d) (e)

BUILD UP EXERCISES

Carwen Products Welsh Sector Report

Last year Carwen Products continued to offer specialist products to every sector of the market. However, the largest proportion of our sales is to the retail sector.

Market share remains higher than that of our closest competitors (details below).

COMPANY	LOCATION
Salisbury Sales	Cardiff
Ingres Interiors	Bristol
Trend Setters	Birmingham
Petra Fabrics	Leeds

SALESFORCE

Our salesforce offers years of experience, product and market knowledge, and continues to develop business.

> Insert the PIE CHART here. Ensure it is legible and is displayed within the margins

5.2(c)

5.4(i)

It possesses the latest details regarding service information. Many staff have increased sales with their key accounts.

NEW PAGE

5.4(k)

OBJECTIVES

TRANSPORT

Double line spacing for this section

Our decision to introduce company vans has provided increased benefits. We now

provide a local delivery service twice weekly, with many areas served three times weekly.

Deliveries are supported by carrier services, and a 24 hour delivery service. The

following customers have expressed their satisfaction with this new service:

5.4(d)

> Insert the DATABASE extract here, using the format specified for this document including character size and line spacing

5.2(a)
5.4(i)

BRANCH NETWORK

Our network continues to thrive. Carwen Products have developed an experienced,

knowledgeable staff throughout the country to provide a local, direct service, a product

range second to none, and vast stockholding.

STOCKHOLDING AND PRODUCT RANGE

We hold an extensive product range across our branches, at generous levels, to satisfy

local needs immediately.

NEW PAGE

5.4(k)

We have been working on a collection of accessories, and the following items will be

added to our catalogue which will be circulated next month.

BUILD UP EXERCISES

1   CURTAIN POLES

A premier collection of made-to-measure curtain poles in polished and lacquered

solid brass, natural, stained and painted wood.

2   TRIMMINGS COLLECTION

This collection includes curtain tiebacks (in reels or cut to length service). We

offer 18 rich colourways and 11 trim options.

3   CURTAIN ACCESSORIES AND PRE-PACKAGED POLES

We offer a range of decorative curtain accessories - solid brass tassel hooks and

holdbacks, holdbacks in marble and ceramics, a colourful range of tassel

tiebacks, and solid brass coronas. We also include a range of wood and brass

curtain poles.

SUPPLIER RELATIONSHIPS

Please note the graph for supplier sales in 1994.

We continue to develop excellent working relationships with our suppliers. The sales

figures below show the values from the graph of supplier sales (1994).

Insert the SPREADSHEET extract here,
using the format specified for this document,
including character size

5.2(b)
5.4(i)

TASK 2

What is this task for?

This task is designed to allow you to practise some of the skills required to gain IBTII assessment objectives

| 5.1 | **Retrieve previously stored document** |

| 5.3 | **Amend documents** |
insert data
delete data
move data
replace data

| 5.5 | **Save file** |

| 5.6 | **Copy file** |

| 5.7 | **Record file storage details** |

| 5.8 | **Print document** |

Before you begin

You will need to find out and note down how to:

- amend documents
  insert data
  delete data
  move data
  replace data
- copy file.

There is a checklist for you to complete on page 51 to use as a reference sheet.

		OBJECTIVES
1	Reload the file saved in Task 1.	
2	Amend the file as indicated, retaining the file specification from Task 1.	**5.4(a) (b) (c) (d) (e) (f) (g) (h)**
3	If necessary, resize the pie chart and repaginate. Save the file using a unique filename, and record the details on the File Store Record Sheet. Make a copy of your amended file, and record the details on the File Store Record Sheet.	**5.4(i) (j) (l) 5.5(a) (b) 5.6(a) 5.7(a)**
4	Print the document on A4 paper.	**5.8(a) (b) (c) (d) (e)**

BUILD UP EXERCISES

Carwen Products Welsh Sector Report

Last year Carwen Products continued to offer specialist products to every sector of the market. ~~However, the largest proportion of our sales is to the retail sector.~~ ← [delete]

Market share remains higher than that of our closest competitors (details below). We retained 30% and hope to increase that share to 40% this year.

COMPANY	LOCATION
Salisbury Sales	Cardiff
Ingres Interiors	Bristol
Trend Setters	Birmingham
Petra Fabrics	Leeds

SALESFORCE

very many

Our salesforce offers /years of experience, product and market knowledge, and continues to develop business.

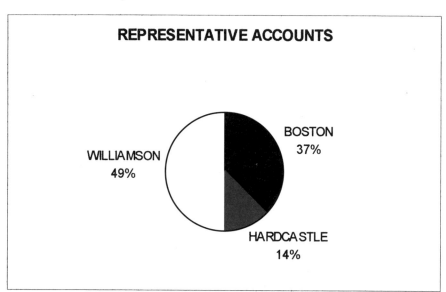

REPRESENTATIVE ACCOUNTS

BOSTON 37%
WILLIAMSON 49%
HARDCASTLE 14%

It possesses the latest details regarding service information.   Many staff have increased sales with their ~~key~~ accounts. [delete]

[*]

Move the BRANCH NETWORK text to this position

BUILD UP EXERCISES

TRANSPORT

to our customers

Our decision to introduce company vans has provided increased benefits/ We now provide a local delivery service twice weekly, with many areas served three times weekly. Deliveries are supported by carrier services, and a 24 hour delivery service. The following customers have expressed their satisfaction with this new service:

5.3(a)

SUPNAME	SUPLOC	CUSTCON	REP
ANDERSON	BATH	TYSON	HARDCASTLE
DEWAR	SHEFFIELD	PALMER	WILLIAMSON
ABBOT	BOLTON	GRIMES	BOSTON
REYNOLDS	HUDDERSFIELD	PATERSON	WILLIAMSON
PORTER	BRADFORD	GRACE	BOSTON
ANDERSON	BATH	FORRESTER	WILLIAMSON

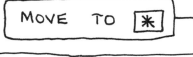

MOVE TO ✱

BRANCH NETWORK

Our network continues to thrive. Carwen Products have developed an experienced, knowledgeable staff throughout the country to provide a local, direct service, ~~a product range second to none~~, and vast stockholding. *delete*

5.3(b) (c)

STOCKHOLDING AND PRODUCT RANGE

We hold an extensive product range across our branches, at generous levels, to satisfy local needs immediately.

NEW PAGE

5.4(k)

BUILD UP EXERCISES

PLANS FOR THE FORTHCOMING YEAR

We have been working on a collection of accessories, and the following items will be added to our new / catalogue which will be circulated next month.

5.3(a)

1   CURTAIN POLES

A premier collection of made-to-measure curtain poles in polished and lacquered solid brass, natural, stained and painted wood, *with a 5 day delivery promise.*

5.3(a)

2   TRIMMINGS COLLECTION

This collection includes curtain tiebacks (in reels or cut to length service). We offer 18 rich colourways and 11 trim options.

3   CURTAIN ACCESSORIES AND PRE-PACKAGED POLES

We offer a range of decorative curtain accessories - solid brass tassel hooks and holdbacks, holdbacks in marble and ceramics, a colourful range of tassel tiebacks, and solid brass coronas. We also include a range of wood and brass curtain poles.

SUPPLIER RELATIONSHIPS

~~Please note the graph for supplier sales in 1994.~~ ◄ *delete*

5.3(b)

We continue to develop excellent working relationships with our suppliers. The sales figures below show the values from the graph of supplier sales (1994).

SUPPLIER CODE	SUPPLIER TOTAL
AB93	
	3939.00
AN12	
	12285.00
DE86	4180.00
PT55	8281.00
RE20	8240.00
WH17	10540.00

Replace the word Carwen with the word Stallman throughout this document

5.3(d)

INTEGRATE FILES AND PRESENT A DOCUMENT CHECKLIST

You should complete this checklist for each hardware and software combination you use. Use information from your tutor, handouts, handbooks and software manuals to complete the list. You can then use your list as a reference sheet to complete the practice task that follows.

IBTII REF	ASSESSMENT OBJECTIVE	HOW TO DO IT
5.1	Retrieve previously stored document	_____
5.2	Import information from	
	database	_____
	spreadsheet	_____
	pie chart	_____
	bar chart	_____
5.3	Amend documents	
	insert data	_____
	delete data	_____
	move data	_____
	replace data	_____
5.4	Format information	
	set top margin	_____
	set left margin	_____
	set line length	_____
	set line spacing	_____
	set justification ON/OFF	_____
	control page numbers	_____
	position page numbers	_____
	set character size	_____
	re-size graphical representation	_____
	insert page breaks	_____
	repaginate	_____
5.5	Save file	_____
5.6	Copy file	_____
5.7	Record file storage details	_____
5.8	Print document	_____

FULL PRACTICE ASSIGNMENT

TASK 3

What's this task for?

This task is designed to allow you to practise a complete assignment. It covers all the IBTII Integrate Files and Present a Document assessment objectives. You **cannot** use this assignment for assessment purposes.

OBJECTIVES

Use the details on your File Store Record Sheet to recall the following files:

APPLICATION	TASK	PRINT
Word Processing	4	1
Database	4	3
Spreadsheet	4	3
Graphics (BAR CHART)	3	2

You are required to prepare the final document using your Word Processing assignment file. Recall the file and amend it as shown incorporating the extracts you produced in the Database and Spreadsheet assignments, and the bar chart from the Graphics assignment, as indicated on pages 53–55.

Please ensure that the format specification covers the Database and Spreadsheet extracts of your document. The graphical representation must be legible and displayed within the margins.

---

1 Recall your Word Processing assignment and use the specification below to produce the final document:

Top margin	Not less than 1.3 cm ($\frac{1}{2}$")	
Left margin	Not less than 1.3 cm ($\frac{1}{2}$")	
Line length	16.5 cm ($6\frac{1}{2}$")	
Line spacing	Single (except where indicated)	
Alignment	Left aligned, ragged right	
Character size	12 point or 12 cpi (decrease size)	
Paper size	A4	
Paper numbers	Bottom centre. Start at page 6.	

5.1(a)

5.4(a)
5.4(b)
5.4(c)
5.4(d)
5.4(e)
5.4(h)
5.8(d)
5.4(f) (g)

---

2 Amend your file as indicated. If necessary, resize the bar chart and repaginate. Save the amended file using a unique filename. Make a copy of your file using a unique filename, and record the details of both on the File Store Record Sheet.

5.4(i) (j) (l)
5.5(a) (b)
5.6(a)
5.7(a)

---

3 Print the document on A4 paper.

5.8(a) (b) (c)

(d) (e)

FULL PRACTICE ASSIGNMENT

CUSTOMER CARE CENTRE ENQUIRY

In the last year we have received a number of complaints regarding our products. The majority have been from our southern area. *I would be grateful if you could deal with this enquiry.*
This is of considerable concern as the south is the highest yield area. I have provided a profile of sales for your information.

> *Insert the BAR CHART here. Ensure it is legible and is displayed within the margins.*

The chart is a useful guide, but I also include data below which gives you a breakdown of the sales figures. ~~Your representatives~~

~~Wade~~
~~Weston~~
~~Davis~~
~~Cole~~
~~Hill~~
~~Winter~~

delete

~~have performed extremely well, but we have received too many complaints.~~

> *Insert the SPREADSHEET extract here, using the format specified for this document, including character size*

FULL PRACTICE ASSIGNMENT

I would be grateful if you would provide me with an analysis of these problems. Are there any areas of similarity? Was the product provided by any one supplier?

Was there a faulty batch supplied?

5.3(a)

NEW PAGE

5.4(k)

NEW PRODUCT DEVELOPMENT

I have attached the text for our new advertising leaflet. Please discuss it with your representatives, and return any comments by the end of the week.

and their contacts

5.4(d)
5.3(a)

The chart below gives a breakdown of customers by area.

I believe we should use the following customers to provide the first series of outlets for the new flooring:

This section ONLY in double line spacing

Insert the DATABASE extract here, using the format specified for this document including character size and line spacing

5.2(a)

NEW PAGE PLEASE

5.4(k)

FULL PRACTICE ASSIGNMENT

OBJECTIVES

5.3(a)

Larin Duro from Katell is the next generation of flooring for the home. *Now is the time to try this dynamic new innovation.*
A highly resilient surface, perfectly balanced by a classical printed base design - the result is an outstanding, multi-dimensional effect. It has a wonderfully hard wearing, easy to clean surface.

Larin Duro allows you to obtain a seamless finish in virtually every room. We are happy to accommodate customised orders. The standard range of colourways and widths follows:

COLOUR	WIDTH (METRES)
SILVER SHIMMER	4.75
LIVELY LAVENDER	4.5
BRONZED EARTH	4.25
FREE FOREST	4
MOONSTONE FIRE	3.75
CHILLED CHERRY	3.5

Ensure that your next flooring has our quality certification. Up to now a dried-in stain on flooring was something you had to live with. With this new concept you can have stain resistance never achieved before.

MOVE

Larin Duro has anti-static control that will last the life of the flooring, which means no more startling shocks, ever!

5.3(c)

This is a completely new way of looking at flooring - take a look for yourself. Call 01552 2569933 for details of your nearest stockist.

Change Larin Duro to Anode Quartz throughout this document

5.3(d)

CUSTOMER

NAME	BRIDGE
COMPANY	MORRIS JONES
ADDRESS	10 CASTLE STREET
TOWN	CHESTER
TELEPHONE	
AREA CODE	01244
NO	75432
TRANSPORT	VAN
SUPPLIER	NEROL
SUPPLIER CODE	NE25
LOCATION	LEEK

PRODUCT CATEGORY

	CARPET		CURTAINING	
	CODE	SQ METRES	CODE	METRES
	SHB1	260	CC9	
	SRB2	500	CS10	
	STHB3	620	AC11	
	STRB4	850	AS12	
	CE5	850	PC13	
	T6	120	PS14	
REPRESENTATIVE			JONES	
AREA			NORTH	
INSTALLATION DATE			30 SEP 94	

CUSTOMER

NAME	EWLOW
COMPANY	HANLEY CARPETS
ADDRESS	6 WILLOW STREET
TOWN	DERBY
TELEPHONE	
AREA CODE	01332
NO	97321
TRANSPORT	VAN
SUPPLIER	NEROL
SUPPLIER CODE	NE25
LOCATION	LEEK

PRODUCT CATEGORY

	CARPET		CURTAINING	
	CODE	SQ METRES	CODE	METRES
	SHB1	295	CC9	
	SRB2	450	CS10	
	STHB3	625	AC11	
	STRB4	1200	AS12	
	CE5	1250	PC13	
	T6	2000	PS14	
REPRESENTATIVE			HARRIS	
AREA			CENTRAL	
INSTALLATION DATE			21 APR 95	

CUSTOMER

NAME	REDDISH
COMPANY	CASTLE CURTAINS
ADDRESS	300 WESTWOOD ROAD
TOWN	EXETER
TELEPHONE	
AREA CODE	01392
NO	76530
TRANSPORT	CARRIER
SUPPLIER	REYNOLDS
SUPPLIER CODE	RE20
LOCATION	HUDDERSFIELD

PRODUCT CATEGORY

	CARPET		CURTAINING	
	CODE	SQ METRES	CODE	METRES
	SHB1		CC9	
	SRB2		CS10	
	STHB3		AC11	490
	STRB4		AS12	
	CE5		PC13	
	T6		PS14	
REPRESENTATIVE			WESTON	
AREA			SOUTH	
INSTALLATION DATE			10 SEP 94	

CUSTOMER

NAME	ANDREW
COMPANY	CARPET CENTRE
ADDRESS	6 KING STREET
TOWN	BRIGHTON
TELEPHONE	
AREA CODE	01273
NO	54887
TRANSPORT	CARRIER
SUPPLIER	DONLAN
SUPPLIER CODE	DN84
LOCATION	MEOLS

PRODUCT CATEGORY

	CARPET		CURTAINING	
CODE	SQ METRES		CODE	METRES
SHB1	650		CC9	
SRB2	720		CS10	
STHB3	800		AC11	
STRB4	895		AS12	
CE5	1000		PC13	
T6	490		PS14	
REPRESENTATIVE			DAVIS	
AREA			SOUTH	
INSTALLATION DATE			7 OCT 94	

CUSTOMER

NAME	GRIFFITHS
COMPANY	J T UPHOLSTERY
ADDRESS	VILLAGE WAY
TOWN	BRISTOL
TELEPHONE	
AREA CODE	01272
NO	53447
TRANSPORT	VAN
SUPPLIER	ANDERSON
SUPPLIER CODE	AN12
LOCATION	BATH

PRODUCT CATEGORY

	CARPET		CURTAINING	
CODE	SQ METRES		CODE	METRES
SHB1			CC9	
SRB2			CS10	450
STHB3			AC11	
STRB4			AS12	
CE5			PC13	
T6			PS14	
REPRESENTATIVE			WADE	
AREA			SOUTH	
INSTALLATION DATE			2 JUN 94	

CUSTOMER

NAME	CLARKE
COMPANY	CARPET TOWN
ADDRESS	30 BURDEN ROAD
TOWN	BRISTOL
TELEPHONE	
AREA CODE	01272
NO	55341
TRANSPORT	VAN
SUPPLIER	MANTEN
SUPPLIER CODE	MA46
LOCATION	BEDFORD

PRODUCT CATEGORY

	CARPET		CURTAINING	
CODE	SQ METRES		CODE	METRES
SHB1	720		CC9	
SRB2	900		CS10	
STHB3	900		AC11	
STRB4	890		AS12	
CE5	650		PC13	
T6	300		PS14	
REPRESENTATIVE			COLE	
AREA			SOUTH	
INSTALLATION DATE			4 DEC 94	

CUSTOMER

NAME	COWAN
COMPANY	CARPET TOWN
ADDRESS	BEVERLEY ROAD
TOWN	HULL
TELEPHONE	
AREA CODE	01482
NO	00750
TRANSPORT	CARRIER
SUPPLIER	DONLAN
SUPPLIER CODE	DN84
LOCATION	MEOLS

PRODUCT CATEGORY

	CARPET		CURTAINING	
CODE	SQ METRES		CODE	METRES
SHB1	690		CC9	
SRB2	600		CS10	
STHB3	620		AC11	
STRB4	850		AS12	
CE5	850		PC13	
T6	220		PS14	
REPRESENTATIVE			WILLIAMS	
AREA			NORTH	
INSTALLATION DATE			18 MAY 94	

CUSTOMER

NAME	JONES
COMPANY	CARPET TILES
ADDRESS	200 MOLD ROAD
TOWN	WREXHAM
TELEPHONE	
AREA CODE	01324
NO	61936
TRANSPORT	CARRIER
SUPPLIER	WYNE
SUPPLIER CODE	WY93
LOCATION	CORWEN

PRODUCT CATEGORY

	CARPET		CURTAINING	
CODE	SQ METRES		CODE	METRES
SHB1	540		CC9	
SRB2	320		CS10	
STHB3	250		AC11	
STRB4	850		AS12	
CE5	850		PC13	
T6	430		PS14	
REPRESENTATIVE			WILLIAMSON	
AREA			WALES	
INSTALLATION DATE			18 APR 93	

CUSTOMER

NAME	BUSSIN
COMPANY	ALLIED GROUP
ADDRESS	18 GLENALMOND ROAD
TOWN	LINCOLN
TELEPHONE	
AREA CODE	01522
NO	65220
TRANSPORT	VAN
SUPPLIER	NEROL
SUPPLIER CODE	NE25
LOCATION	LEEK

PRODUCT CATEGORY

	CARPET		CURTAINING	
CODE	SQ METRES		CODE	METRES
SHB1	400		CC9	
SRB2	520		CS10	
STHB3	200		AC11	
STRB4	1000		AS12	
CE5	490		PC13	
T6	0		PS14	
REPRESENTATIVE			JONES	
AREA			NORTH	
INSTALLATION DATE			9 FEB 93	

CUSTOMER

NAME	FORD
COMPANY	COUNT CARPETS
ADDRESS	144 DUKE STREET
TOWN	EXETER
TELEPHONE	
AREA CODE	01392
NO	83233
TRANSPORT	VAN
SUPPLIER	MANTEN
SUPPLIER CODE	MA46
LOCATION	BEDFORD

PRODUCT CATEGORY

CARPET		CURTAINING	
CODE	SQ METRES	CODE	METRES
SHB1	680	CC9	
SRB2	755	CS10	
STHB3	295	AC11	
STRB4	435	AS12	
CE5	690	PC13	
T6	420	PS14	
REPRESENTATIVE		HILL	
AREA		SOUTH	
INSTALLATION DATE		6 DEC 94	

CUSTOMER

NAME	STOREY
COMPANY	STOREY CARPETS
ADDRESS	STANDARD AVENUE
TOWN	SWANSEA
TELEPHONE	
AREA CODE	01792
NO	46219
TRANSPORT	VAN
SUPPLIER	NEROL
SUPPLIER CODE	NE 25
LOCATION	LEEK

PRODUCT CATEGORY

CARPET		CURTAINING	
CODE	SQ METRES	CODE	METRES
SHB1	200	CC9	
SRB2	290	CS10	
STHB3	325	AC11	
STRB4	480	AS12	
CE5	650	PC13	
T6	100	PS14	
REPRESENTATIVE		BOSTON	
AREA		WALES	
INSTALLATION DATE		2 JAN 93	

CUSTOMER

NAME	MILLER
COMPANY	RENROSE RUGS
ADDRESS	50 WREN PLACE
TOWN	OXFORD
TELEPHONE	
AREA CODE	01865
NO	42212
TRANSPORT	VAN
SUPPLIER	MANTEN
SUPPLIER CODE	MA46
LOCATION	BEDFORD

PRODUCT CATEGORY

CARPET		CURTAINING	
CODE	SQ METRES	CODE	METRES
SHB1	240	CC9	
SRB2	120	CS10	
STHB3	690	AC11	
STRB4	800	AS12	
CE5	300	PC13	
T6	200	PS14	
REPRESENTATIVE		WINTER	
AREA		SOUTH	
INSTALLATION DATE		20 APR 94	

CUSTOMER

NAME	STAHL
COMPANY	CURTAIN CARE
ADDRESS	45 TRANTON ROAD
TOWN	TAUNTON
TELEPHONE	
AREA CODE	01823
NO	43200
TRANSPORT	VAN
SUPPLIER	ABBOT
SUPPLIER CODE	AB93
LOCATION	BOLTON

PRODUCT CATEGORY

	CARPET		CURTAINING	
CODE	SQ METRES		CODE	METRES
SHB1			CC9	
SRB2			CS10	
STHB3			AC11	
STRB4			AS12	
CE5			PC13	
T6			PS14	100
REPRESENTATIVE			WADE	
AREA			SOUTH	
INSTALLATION DATE			5 OCT 94	

CUSTOMER

NAME	SHAW
COMPANY	NOKES ROYAL
ADDRESS	72 URDALL AVENUE
TOWN	WAKEFIELD
TELEPHONE	
AREA CODE	01924
NO	56831
TRANSPORT	VAN
SUPPLIER	NEROL
SUPPLIER CODE	NE25
LOCATION	LEEK

PRODUCT CATEGORY

	CARPET		CURTAINING	
CODE	SQ METRES		CODE	METRES
SHB1	250		CC9	
SRB2	900		CS10	
STHB3	420		AC11	
STRB4	290		AS12	
CE5	1000		PC13	
T6	0		PS14	
REPRESENTATIVE			JONES	
AREA			NORTH	
INSTALLATION DATE			12 APR 95	

CUSTOMER

NAME	MILLER
COMPANY	MILLER BROWN
ADDRESS	39 VENTNOR VILLAS
TOWN	BRIGHTON
TELEPHONE	
AREA CODE	01273
NO	73925
TRANSPORT	CARRIER
SUPPLIER	DEWAR
SUPPLIER CODE	DE86
LOCATION	SHEFFIELD

PRODUCT CATEGORY

	CARPET		CURTAINING	
CODE	SQ METRES		CODE	METRES
SHB1			CC9	195
SRB2			CS10	
STHB3			AC11	
STRB4			AS12	
CE5			PC13	
T6			PS14	
REPRESENTATIVE			WESTON	
AREA			SOUTH	
INSTALLATION DATE			9 FEB 94	

CUSTOMER

NAME	TRENCH
COMPANY	CARPET COMPANY
ADDRESS	THE LAURELS
TOWN	RUTHIN
TELEPHONE	
AREA CODE	01239
NO	64233
TRANSPORT	VAN
SUPPLIER	NEROL
SUPPLIER CODE	NE 25
LOCATION	LEEK

PRODUCT CATEGORY

	CARPET		CURTAINING	
CODE	SQ METRES		CODE	METRES
SHB1	655		CC9	
SRB2	715		CS10	
STHB3	770		AC11	
STRB4	840		AS12	
CE5	925		PC13	
T6	465		PS14	
REPRESENTATIVE			WILLIAMSON	
AREA			WALES	
INSTALLATION DATE			2 JAN 92	

CUSTOMER

NAME	CLARKE
COMPANY	PERFECTION
ADDRESS	24 GLEN LANE
TOWN	LEICESTER
TELEPHONE	
AREA CODE	01533
NO	85453
TRANSPORT	24 - HOUR
SUPPLIER	ABBOT
SUPPLIER CODE	AB93
LOCATION	BOLTON

PRODUCT CATEGORY

	CARPET		CURTAINING	
CODE	SQ METRES		CODE	METRES
SHB1			CC9	
SRB2			CS10	
STHB3			AC11	
STRB4			AS12	
CE5			PC13	
T6			PS14	250
REPRESENTATIVE			HARRIS	
AREA			CENTRAL	
INSTALLATION DATE			1 FEB 95	

CUSTOMER

NAME	DART
COMPANY	THE LINEN SHOP
ADDRESS	62 HINTON WAY
TOWN	OXFORD
TELEPHONE	
AREA CODE	01865
NO	41141
TRANSPORT	24 - HOUR
SUPPLIER	REYNOLDS
SUPPLIER CODE	RE20
LOCATION	HUDDERSFIELD

PRODUCT CATEGORY

	CARPET		CURTAINING	
CODE	SQ METRES		CODE	METRES
SHB1			CC9	
SRB2			CS10	
STHB3			AC11	500
STRB4			AS12	
CE5			PC13	
T6			PS14	
REPRESENTATIVE			HILL	
AREA			SOUTH	
INSTALLATION DATE			4 AUG 94	

CUSTOMER

NAME	OHAJURU
COMPANY	CURTAIN FACTORY
ADDRESS	2 WELWYN WAY
TOWN	PRESTON
TELEPHONE	
AREA CODE	01772
NO	83280
TRANSPORT	CARRIER
SUPPLIER	DEWAR
SUPPLIER CODE	DE86
LOCATION	SHEFFIELD

PRODUCT CATEGORY

CARPET		CURTAINING	
CODE	SQ METRES	CODE	METRES
SHB1		CC9	125
SRB2		CS10	
STHB3		AC11	
STRB4		AS12	
CE5		PC13	
T6		PS14	

REPRESENTATIVE	JONES
AREA	NORTH
INSTALLATION DATE	4 MAY 92

CUSTOMER

NAME	WILLIAMS
COMPANY	THE CARPET SHOP
ADDRESS	256 FINDLAY ROAD
TOWN	CARDIFF
TELEPHONE	
AREA CODE	01222
NO	47832
TRANSPORT	VAN
SUPPLIER	MANTEN
SUPPLIER CODE	MA46
LOCATION	BEDFORD

PRODUCT CATEGORY

CARPET		CURTAINING	
CODE	SQ METRES	CODE	METRES
SHB1	650	CC9	
SRB2	720	CS10	
STHB3	800	AC11	
STRB4	895	AS12	
CE5	1000	PC13	
T6	105	PS14	

REPRESENTATIVE	BOSTON
AREA	WALES
INSTALLATION DATE	29 SEP 92

CUSTOMER

NAME	FEINNE
COMPANY	CONCEPTS
ADDRESS	27 CROATEN ROAD
TOWN	READING
TELEPHONE	
AREA CODE	01734
NO	63500
TRANSPORT	VAN
SUPPLIER	ANDERSON
SUPPLIER CODE	AN12
LOCATION	BATH

PRODUCT CATEGORY

CARPET		CURTAINING	
CODE	SQ METRES	CODE	METRES
SHB1		CC9	
SRB2		CS10	400
STHB3		AC11	
STRB4		AS12	
CE5		PC13	
T6		PS14	

REPRESENTATIVE	WINTER
AREA	SOUTH
INSTALLATION DATE	25 NOV 94

CUSTOMER

NAME	TAYLOR
COMPANY	CARPET STORE
ADDRESS	46 BAMBURN STREET
TOWN	STAFFORD
TELEPHONE	
AREA CODE	01785
NO	45450
TRANSPORT	VAN
SUPPLIER	NEROL
SUPPLIER CODE	NE25
LOCATION	LEEK

PRODUCT CATEGORY

CARPET		CURTAINING	
CODE	SQ METRES	CODE	METRES
SHB1	450	CC9	
SRB2	490	CS10	
STHB3	535	AC11	
STRB4	580	AS12	
CE5	635	PC13	
T6	260	PS14	
REPRESENTATIVE		WEST	
AREA		CENTRAL	
INSTALLATION DATE		14 SEP 94	

CUSTOMER

NAME	FORREST
COMPANY	BELLS
ADDRESS	57 HENSELL ROAD
TOWN	TELFORD
TELEPHONE	
AREA CODE	01952
NO	32895
TRANSPORT	VAN
SUPPLIER	NEROL
SUPPLIER CODE	NE25
LOCATION	LEEK

PRODUCT CATEGORY

CARPET		CURTAINING	
CODE	SQ METRES	CODE	METRES
SHB1	155	CC9	
SRB2	165	CS10	
STHB3	180	AC11	
STRB4	200	AS12	
CE5	320	PC13	
T6	340	PS14	
REPRESENTATIVE		HARRIS	
AREA		CENTRAL	
INSTALLATION DATE		8 JULY 94	

CUSTOMER

NAME	CROSBY
COMPANY	CURTAIN CALL
ADDRESS	31 EASTWICK ROAD
TOWN	WARWICK
TELEPHONE	
AREA CODE	01926
NO	05432
TRANSPORT	VAN
SUPPLIER	WHITAKER
SUPPLIER CODE	WH17
LOCATION	CHESTER

PRODUCT CATEGORY

CARPET		CURTAINING	
CODE	SQ METRES	CODE	METRES
SHB1		CC9	
SRB2		CS10	
STHB3		AC11	
STRB4		AS12	100
CE5		PC13	
T6		PS14	
REPRESENTATIVE		WEST	
AREA		CENTRAL	
INSTALLATION DATE		9 MAR 95	

CUSTOMER

NAME	JOHNSON
COMPANY	CARPETS GALORE
ADDRESS	10 BRIDGE STREET
TOWN	EXETER
TELEPHONE	
AREA CODE	01392
NO	21140
TRANSPORT	CARRIER
SUPPLIER	WYNE
SUPPLIER CODE	WY93
LOCATION	CORWEN

PRODUCT CATEGORY

CARPET		CURTAINING	
CODE	SQ METRES	CODE	METRES
SHB1	645	CC9	
SRB2	685	CS10	
STHB3	635	AC11	
STRB4	535	AS12	
CE5	590	PC13	
T6	300	PS14	

REPRESENTATIVE	WADE
AREA	SOUTH
INSTALLATION DATE	28 SEP 94

CUSTOMER

NAME	HARRISON
COMPANY	MOLD INTERIORS
ADDRESS	RUTHIN ROAD
TOWN	MOLD
TELEPHONE	
AREA CODE	01352
NO	44238
TRANSPORT	VAN
SUPPLIER	ANDERSON
SUPPLIER CODE	AN12
LOCATION	BATH

PRODUCT CATEGORY

CARPET		CURTAINING	
CODE	SQ METRES	CODE	METRES
SHB1		CC9	
SRB2		CS10	550
STHB3		AC11	
STRB4		AS12	
CE5		PC13	
T6		PS14	

REPRESENTATIVE	HARDCASTLE
AREA	WALES
INSTALLATION DATE	6 MAR 93

CUSTOMER

NAME	BARNES
COMPANY	CARPET CITY
ADDRESS	26 WILLIAM SQUARE
TOWN	BRIGHTON
TELEPHONE	
AREA CODE	01273
NO	72950
TRANSPORT	CARRIER
SUPPLIER	WYNE
SUPPLIER CODE	WY93
LOCATION	CORWEN

PRODUCT CATEGORY

CARPET		CURTAINING	
CODE	SQ METRES	CODE	METRES
SHB1	310	CC9	
SRB2	450	CS10	
STHB3	400	AC11	
STRB4	150	AS12	
CE5	520	PC13	
T6	140	PS14	

REPRESENTATIVE	WESTON
AREA	SOUTH
INSTALLATION DATE	1 APR 94

CUSTOMER

NAME	GRACE
COMPANY	GRACEFUL INTERIORS
ADDRESS	10 THE CUTTINGS
TOWN	SWANSEA
TELEPHONE	
AREA CODE	01792
NO	92133
TRANSPORT	VAN
SUPPLIER	PORTER
SUPPLIER CODE	PT55
LOCATION	BRADFORD

PRODUCT CATEGORY

CARPET		CURTAINING	
CODE	SQ METRES	CODE	METRES
SHB1		CC9	
SRB2		CS10	
STHB3		AC11	
STRB4		AS12	
CE5		PC13	980
T6		PS14	
REPRESENTATIVE		BOSTON	
AREA		WALES	
INSTALLATION DATE		12 DEC 94	

CUSTOMER

NAME	GRIMES
COMPANY	CURTAIN FAIR
ADDRESS	52 SCREED ROAD
TOWN	CARDIFF
TELEPHONE	
AREA CODE	01222
NO	39920
TRANSPORT	VAN
SUPPLIER	ABBOT
SUPPLIER CODE	AB93
LOCATION	BOLTON

PRODUCT CATEGORY

CARPET		CURTAINING	
CODE	SQ METRES	CODE	METRES
SHB1		CC9	
SRB2		CS10	
STHB3		AC11	
STRB4		AS12	
CE5		PC13	
T6		PS14	255
REPRESENTATIVE		BOSTON	
AREA		WALES	
INSTALLATION DATE		11 OCT 94	

CUSTOMER

NAME	FORRESTER
COMPANY	FORRESTERS
ADDRESS	420 BRANDON STREET
TOWN	SWANSEA
TELEPHONE	
AREA CODE	01792
NO	20341
TRANSPORT	VAN
SUPPLIER	ANDERSON
SUPPLIER CODE	AN12
LOCATION	BATH

PRODUCT CATEGORY

CARPET		CURTAINING	
CODE	SQ METRES	CODE	METRES
SHB1		CC9	
SRB2		CS10	800
STHB3		AC11	
STRB4		AS12	
CE5		PC13	
T6		PS14	
REPRESENTATIVE		WILLIAMSON	
AREA		WALES	
INSTALLATION DATE		21 DEC 94	

CUSTOMER

NAME	BUTLER
COMPANY	BUTLER & JONES
ADDRESS	10 GREAT COATES LANE
TOWN	CARDIFF
TELEPHONE	
AREA CODE	01222
NO	13920
TRANSPORT	CARRIER
SUPPLIER	WHITAKER
SUPPLIER CODE	WH17
LOCATION	CHESTER

PRODUCT CATEGORY

CARPET		CURTAINING	
CODE	SQ METRES	CODE	METRES
SHB1		CC9	
SRB2		CS10	
STHB3		AC11	
STRB4		AS12	1240
CE5		PC13	
T6		PS14	

REPRESENTATIVE	BOSTON
AREA	WALES
INSTALLATION DATE	15 NOV 94

CUSTOMER

NAME	PALMER
COMPANY	PALM COURTS
ADDRESS	10 COURT STREET
TOWN	CORWEN
TELEPHONE	
AREA CODE	01490
NO	42335
TRANSPORT	VAN
SUPPLIER	DEWAR
SUPPLIER CODE	DE86
LOCATION	SHEFFIELD

PRODUCT CATEGORY

CARPET		CURTAINING	
CODE	SQ METRES	CODE	METRES
SHB1		CC9	400
SRB2		CS10	
STHB3		AC11	
STRB4		AS12	
CE5		PC13	
T6		PS14	

REPRESENTATIVE	WILLIAMSON
AREA	WALES
INSTALLATION DATE	8 SEP 94

CUSTOMER

NAME	DOWLING
COMPANY	DOWLING BROS
ADDRESS	44 HIGH STREET
TOWN	BALA
TELEPHONE	
AREA CODE	01678
NO	89422
TRANSPORT	VAN
SUPPLIER	WHITAKER
SUPPLIER CODE	WH17
LOCATION	CHESTER

PRODUCT CATEGORY

CARPET		CURTAINING	
CODE	SQ METRES	CODE	METRES
SHB1		CC9	
SRB2		CS10	
STHB3		AC11	
STRB4		AS12	750
CE5		PC13	
T6		PS14	

REPRESENTATIVE	HARDCASTLE
AREA	WALES
INSTALLATION DATE	3 MAY 95

CUSTOMER

NAME	CRAVEN
COMPANY	LANGPORTS
ADDRESS	CHANNEL COURT
TOWN	BALA
TELEPHONE	
AREA CODE	01678
NO	23590
TRANSPORT	VAN
SUPPLIER	PORTER
SUPPLIER CODE	PT55
LOCATION	BRADFORD

PRODUCT CATEGORY

	CARPET		CURTAINING	
CODE	SQ METRES		CODE	METRES
SHB1			CC9	
SRB2			CS10	
STHB3			AC11	
STRB4			AS12	
CE5			PC13	255
T6			PS14	
REPRESENTATIVE			HARDCASTLE	
AREA			WALES	
INSTALLATION DATE			4 JUN 95	

CUSTOMER

NAME	TYSON
COMPANY	TYSON BROS
ADDRESS	22 CARDIGAN PLACE
TOWN	RUTHIN
TELEPHONE	
AREA CODE	01824
NO	33342
TRANSPORT	VAN
SUPPLIER	ANDERSON
SUPPLIER CODE	AN12
LOCATION	BATH

PRODUCT CATEGORY

	CARPET		CURTAINING	
CODE	SQ METRES		CODE	METRES
SHB1			CC9	
SRB2			CS10	500
STHB3			AC11	
STRB4			AS12	
CE5			PC13	
T6			PS14	
REPRESENTATIVE			HARDCASTLE	
AREA			WALES	
INSTALLATION DATE			6 APR 94	

CUSTOMER

NAME	DEAN
COMPANY	DEAN & WILLIAMS
ADDRESS	22 WELMORE ROAD
TOWN	CORWEN
TELEPHONE	
AREA CODE	01490
NO	92741
TRANSPORT	24 – HOUR
SUPPLIER	ABBOT
SUPPLIER CODE	AB93
LOCATION	BOLTON

PRODUCT CATEGORY

	CARPET		CURTAINING	
CODE	SQ METRES		CODE	METRES
SHB1			CC9	
SRB2			CS10	
STHB3			AC11	
STRB4			AS12	
CE5			PC13	
T6			PS14	250
REPRESENTATIVE			WILLIAMSON	
AREA			WALES	
INSTALLATION DATE			26 AUG 94	

CUSTOMER

NAME	HOLMES
COMPANY	HAPPY HOLMES
ADDRESS	4 ALBROCH ROAD
TOWN	CARDIFF
TELEPHONE	
AREA CODE	01222
NO	52552
TRANSPORT	CARRIER
SUPPLIER	PORTER
SUPPLIER CODE	PT55
LOCATION	BRADFORD

PRODUCT CATEGORY

CARPET		CURTAINING	
CODE	SQ METRES	CODE	METRES
SHB1		CC9	
SRB2		CS10	
STHB3		AC11	
STRB4		AS12	
CE5		PC13	255
T6		PS14	

REPRESENTATIVE	BOSTON
AREA	WALES
INSTALLATION DATE	12 FEB 95

CUSTOMER

NAME	PATERSON
COMPANY	RILEY & PATERSON
ADDRESS	PRESCOT PLACE
TOWN	ABERYSTWYTH
TELEPHONE	
AREA CODE	01970
NO	81711
TRANSPORT	VAN
SUPPLIER	REYNOLDS
SUPPLIER CODE	RE20
LOCATION	HUDDERSFIELD

PRODUCT CATEGORY

CARPET		CURTAINING	
CODE	SQ METRES	CODE	METRES
SHB1		CC9	
SRB2		CS10	
STHB3		AC11	800
STRB4		AS12	
CE5		PC13	
T6		PS14	

REPRESENTATIVE	WILLIAMSON
AREA	WALES
INSTALLATION DATE	23 OCT 94

CUSTOMER

NAME	OWEN
COMPANY	OWEN DESIGNS
ADDRESS	20 MARKET STREET
TOWN	MOLD
TELEPHONE	
AREA CODE	01352
NO	55255
TRANSPORT	24 – HOUR
SUPPLIER	REYNOLDS
SUPPLIER CODE	RE 20
LOCATION	HUDDERSFIELD

PRODUCT CATEGORY

CARPET		CURTAINING	
CODE	SQ METRES	CODE	METRES
SHB1		CC9	
SRB2		CS10	
STHB3		AC11	150
STRB4		AS12	
CE5		PC13	
T6		PS14	

REPRESENTATIVE	HARDCASTLE
AREA	WALES
INSTALLATION DATE	19 FEB 95

The material costs are shown as follows:

1 Carpet range – cost per square metre.

2 Curtain range – cost per metre.

CODE	DESCRIPTION	1992	1993	1994	1995
	CARPET RANGE				
SHB1	Supreme Hessian Back	14.50	15.50	15.75	16.25
SRB2	Supreme Rubber Back	12.75	13.00	13.80	14.00
STHB3	Standard Hessian Back	11.50	11.75	12.00	12.30
STRB4	Standard Rubber Back	10.00	10.40	10.95	11.25
CE5	Cord Extra	9.25	9.60	9.90	10.25
T6	Tiles (1square metre)	7.50	7.70	7.90	8.10
AVERAGE COST PER SQUARE METRE		10.92	11.33	11.72	12.02
	CURTAIN RANGE				
CC9	Country Classic	9.75	10.25	10.45	11.00
CS10	Country Standard	8.75	9.20	9.45	9.70
AC11	Abstract Classic	9.50	9.80	10.30	10.75
AS12	Abstract Standard	8.50	8.50	8.50	8.50
PC13	Plain Classic	8.00	8.20	8.45	8.65
PS14	Plain Standard	7.00	7.30	7.80	8.10
AVERAGE COST PER METRE		8.58	8.88	9.16	9.45

Assignments

6

The assignments in this chapter are based on the work of Wirral Security Bureau, a company which operates in the north west of England. The organisation works in conjunction with a number of other agencies and it is essential that communication with them is both rapid and accurate.

The company requires very tight control of its financial monitoring and finance collection services. It also needs to have close control of the status of any of its current work files.

Wirral Security Bureau handles a large number of financial transactions. It is essential that all company records are kept up to date, and that all members of staff have access to the same information, sometimes concurrently.

Norman Southern, the company's Managing Director, first introduced computer systems into the company in 1987, and acknowledges that the company would now have great difficulty operating without them. They are used for keeping control of the client base and for keeping track of the company's income and expenses. Norman also uses the systems to prepare analytical reports on client and job profiles to ensure that the company is moving in the right direction, and to highlight areas that may need consideration and change.

Paula Williams is in charge of the day-to-day running of the financial tracking systems. She updates the client files and keeps other interested parties in touch with case status.

Henry Booth carries out most of the site visits in conjunction with Norman. On site, they record the critical information and transmit it to Paula, who then updates the computer files.

You are to complete some of the work carried out by Paula.

She prepares standard reports for clients following case action.
You are required to provide a document for management that outlines two items:

▪ the results of a visit on behalf of a client
▪ a marketing report.

To prepare the document you will carry out the following set of assignments:

1 DATABASE You will set up a database of client detail records (from 1994 onwards).

2 SPREADSHEET You will prepare a spreadsheet showing costs for 1995. You will enter the current fees and warrant costs and project values for additional costs.

3 WORD PROCESSING You will create a report (to a given specification) outlining the results of a site visit, and also a marketing feature.

4 GRAPHICS You will create a pie chart showing the breakdown of the clients who pay in 1, 2 and 3 years (from 1994 onwards).
You will also prepare a bar chart showing the total amounts due, by year, in 1995.

5 INTEGRATE FILES AND PRESENT A DOCUMENT The fifth assignment involves the preparation of the final document. It will be prepared by amending your Word Processing file, and including extracts from the Database and Spreadsheet assignments and the pie chart from the Graphics assignment, where instructed.

Points for special attention

▪ The format required for the document in assignment 5 covers all sections of that report, i.e. you must apply the format to the sections extracted from the Database and Spreadsheet assignments.

▪ As the final document is a combination of the other assignments, it is advisable to use the same font/typeface for all the assignments. You may use any font/typeface that can be increased by two points. You MUST use the same font/typeface for assignments 3 and 5.

▪ Remember to save with a **unique** filename **each time**.

DATABASE ASSIGNMENT

OBJECTIVES

1 Using the information on the **CLIENT DETAIL CARDS** (pages 84–91), set up a database of client detail records. Ensure that the field width is adjusted to accommodate the data. You must use the following field headings in your reports (a guide is given to the field content):

1.2(a) (c)

1.2(b)

HEADING	FIELD CONTENT
SURNAME	SURNAME
FIRST NAME	FIRST NAME
TOWN	TOWN
DOB	DATE OF BIRTH
DATE	START DATE
YEARS	PAYMENT YEARS
PAY	PAYMENT FREQUENCY using the following codes:
	CODE FREQUENCY
	W WEEKLY
	M MONTHLY
	Q QUARTERLY
AMOUNT	TOTAL AMOUNT DUE

2 Enter the relevant data. You should include **ONLY** the details shown for clients with a **START DATE AFTER 1 JAN 1994**.

1.1(a)
1.3(a) (b)

3 Save the data using a unique filename, and record the details on the File Store Record Sheet.

1.7(a) (d)
1.8(a)

4 Create a report in table format to display **ALL** the records. Use the headings given above. Save the report using a unique filename, and record the details on the File Store Record Sheet.

1.6(a) (d)
1.7(c) (d)
1.8(a)

5 Print the report in table format, including the field headings.

1.9(a) (b) (c)

6 Sort the list into **DESCENDING** order of **AMOUNT**.

1.5(a)

7 Save the list, using a unique filename, in **DESCENDING** order of **AMOUNT**, and record the details on the File Store Record Sheet.

1.7(a)
1.8(a)

8 Create a report in table format, include the field headings, and display the following fields **ONLY**:

SURNAME ▪ **DOB** ▪ **YEARS** ▪ **PAY** ▪ **AMOUNT**

1.6(a) (b)

9 Save the report using a unique filename, and record the details on the File Store Record Sheet.

1.7(c) (d)
1.8(a)

DATABASE ASSIGNMENT

		OBJECTIVES

10 Print the report in table format, including the field headings.

OBJECTIVES 1.9(a) (b) (c)

11 Search for those customers in **BOOTLE** who have agreed to pay **MONTHLY** for **1 YEAR**. Save the list using a unique filename, and record the details on the File Store Record Sheet.

1.4(a)
1.7(b) (d)
1.8(a)

12 Using the search list from 11 above, create a report in table format to display **ONLY** the fields indicated below, in the order shown:

SURNAME ▪ **AMOUNT** ▪ **DATE**

1.6(c) (d)

13 Save the report using a unique filename, and record the details on the File Store Record Sheet. **This report will be used later in assignment 5**.

1.7(c) (d)
1.8(a)

14 Print the report in table format, including the field headings.

1.9(a) (b) (c)

SPREADSHEET ASSIGNMENT

Create a spreadsheet which displays costs for the year 1995. You will enter the current fees and warrant costs and project values for additional costs.

---

1 Enter the title: **1995 COSTS**

Your spreadsheet must include:

2.3(a)

CNO	PAYMENT YEARS	TOTAL AMOUNT DUE	FEES	WARRANT COST	FIRST YEAR
TOTALS					

---

2 Using the information on the **CLIENT DETAIL CARDS** (pages 84–91), enter the text and numeric data for the items shown. Enter the data for all clients with a **START DATE in 1995 ONLY**. Ensure that all text and figures in column 1 are left aligned and that the text and figures in the remaining columns are right aligned. Display all monetary amounts to 2 decimal places, and all other figures in integer format.

2.1(a)
2.2 (a) (b) (c)
(d) (e) (f)
2.3 (a) (b)

---

3 Using the appropriate formula, generate a figure in the **FIRST YEAR** column (TOTAL AMOUNT DUE divided by PAYMENT YEARS) for the first CNO. Replicate this formula for each of the other CNOs.

2.4 (a) (b)

---

4 On the **TOTALS** row, using the appropriate formula, generate a total in the **TOTAL AMOUNT DUE** column. Replicate this formula for the **FEES** and **WARRANT COST** columns.

2.4 (a) (b)

---

5 Save the spreadsheet using a unique filename, and enter the filename on the File Store Record Sheet. Print the spreadsheet.

2.7 (a) (b) (c)
2.8 (a)
2.9 (a) (b) (c)

---

6 Print the headings and data in the **CNO, PAYMENT YEARS** and **TOTAL AMOUNT DUE** columns **ONLY. This extract will be used later in assignment 5.**

2.7 (d)
2.9 (a) (c)

SPREADSHEET ASSIGNMENT

7 Insert a column, headed **EXPENSES 2.5%**, after the column headed **WARRANT COST** and before the column headed **FIRST YEAR**. Use the appropriate formula to generate the amount (2.5% of WARRANT COST) for the first CNO. Replicate this formula for each of the other CNOs.

2.4 (a) (b)
2.5 (a) (b)

8 On the **TOTALS** row, use the appropriate formula to generate a total for the **EXPENSES 2.5%** column you have just inserted. Ensure that both the column heading and figures are right aligned, and that monetary amounts are displayed to 2 decimal places.

2.4 (a)
2.2 (b) (c) (e) (f)

9 Ensure that the formulae in the TOTAL AMOUNT DUE column is amended to include the data in the column you have just inserted.

2.4 (a)

10 Save the spreadsheet using a unique filename, and enter the filename on the File Store Record Sheet. Print the spreadsheet.

2.7 (a) (b) (c)
2.8 (a)
2.9 (a) (b) (c)

11 Change the **EXPENSES** to **5%** of **WARRANT COST**. Ensure that this change is reflected in the heading.

2.6 (a) (b)

12 Save your file using a unique filename, and record the details on the File Store Record Sheet.

2.7 (a) (b) (c)
2.8 (a)

13 Print the spreadsheet.

2.9 (a) (b) (c)

14 Print the spreadsheet **FORMULAE** in the **EXPENSES 5%** and **FIRST YEAR** columns.

2.10 (a)

WORD PROCESSING ASSIGNMENT

1 Create a file to the specification shown below. You may use any font/typeface that can be increased by 2 points. You **MUST** use the same font/typeface for assignment 5 Integrate Files and Present a Document.

Top margin	Not less than 1.3 cm ($\frac{1}{2}$")	3.1(a)
Left margin	Not less than 1.3 cm ($\frac{1}{2}$")	3.1(b)
Line length	12.7 cm (5")	3.1(c)
Line spacing	Double	3.1(d)
Alignment	Left aligned, ragged right margin	3.1(e)
Character size	10 point or 14 cpi	3.1(f)
Paper size	A4	3.10(a)
Page numbers	Top right. Start at page 1.	3.7(a) (b)

2 Enter the text below. Save the file using a unique filename, and record the details on the File Store Record Sheet. Print one copy of the file on A4 paper.

3.2(a)
3.8(a) (b)
3.9(a)
3.10(a) (b) (c)

Warrant No

We attended the premises shown on the warrant, where we obtained walking possession.

When we interviewed the owner we were informed that settlement was not possible, but an offer to repay at £1,000.00 per month (with the first payment immediately) was recorded.

We informed the owner that we would submit the offer to yourselves, and await further instructions.

We look forward to hearing from you regarding this matter.

The relevant reference communications to the Under Sheriff have been forwarded to your Chester Office.

WORD PROCESSING ASSIGNMENT

We have made contact with the solicitors of the owner regarding the above agreement, and they inform us that a cheque regarding the warrant has been forwarded for direction to the warrant account.

When we receive the payment, we will forward the amount (less fees and expenses) to the Under Sheriff's Office.

Should there be any problems regarding this matter we will advise you accordingly.

We recognise that court costs can be a major problem. You may be surprised to learn that we can carry out court action that will result in minimal expense to the company.

We could offer this service to other companies. Using our services an enormous number of court actions have incurred no costs. The majority of cases are brought with clients repaying over 2 years. You will see from the breakdown that over 30% of our current client caseload falls into this category.

WORD PROCESSING ASSIGNMENT

BEFORE ACTION ← [centre]

We operate an all inclusive price before action
This package includes:

[Indent this section 13 mm (½") from left margin] →

- receiving your instructions;
- writing letters;
- dealing with telephone calls from responde
  and/or their solicitors;
- dealing with correspondence;
- forwarding correspondence and messages;
- dealing with payments received;
- a reminder service.

COURT ACTION ← [centre]

Quite simply, the cost of court action where
the proceedings are successful can be zero. Costs
are only incurred if the outstanding amount
is higher than £750. The higher the
outstanding amount, the lower the cost. If
there are many high figure accounts, there
could be greater savings.

[NEW PAGE] If court action is successful the costs are as
follows:

OUTSTANDING AMOUNT	MAXIMUM COST
UNDER £750	£0
£750 – £2000	£60
£1000 – £3000	£55
OVER £3000	£10

[emphasise this line]

GRAPHICS ASSIGNMENT

You will create a pie chart showing the breakdown of the percentages of clients who pay in 1, 2 and 3 years (from the end of 1993).

You will also prepare a bar chart showing the total amounts due, by year (1, 2 and 3), in 1995.

---

1 Using the information on the **CLIENT DETAIL CARDS** (pages 84–91), create a pie chart to show the percentage of customers with a **START DATE AFTER 1 JAN 1994**, who pay in 1, 2 and 3 years. Graph the sales by the number of clients.

4.1(a)
4.2(a)
4.3(a)

---

2 The chart must be titled: **CLIENTS/YEARS**

4.2(e)

---

3 The sectors must be labelled with the number of years **(1, 2 or 3)**, or a legend should be attached to identify the sections. A percentage division should also be shown.

4.2(f)
4.3(c)

---

4 Save the display using a unique filename, and enter the filename on the File Store Record Sheet. **This pie chart will be used later in assignment 5.**

4.4(a) (b) (c)
4.5(a)

---

5 Print the graphical representation in landscape display.

4.6(b) (c)

---

6 Using the information on the **CLIENT DETAIL CARDS** (pages 84–91), create a bar chart to show the total amount due by year (1, 2 and 3).

Use the data for 1995 only, and graph the amounts by year.

4.1(a)
4.2(a)
4.3(a)

---

7 The chart must be titled: **TOTALS DUE – YEARS (1-3)**

4.2(b)

---

8 The X axis must be labelled: **NO OF YEARS**

4.2(c)

---

9 The Y axis must be labelled: **AMOUNT (£)**

4.2(c)

---

10 The Y axis scale must be: MIN: **0**
MAX: **45,000**

4.3(b)

---

11 The bars (variables) must be labelled with the NO OF YEARS (1, 2 and 3).

4.2(d)

---

12 Save the display using a unique filename, and enter the filename on the File Store Record Sheet.

4.4(a) (b) (c)
4.5(a)

---

13 Print the graphical representation in portrait display.

4.6(a) (c)

INTEGRATE FILES AND PRESENT A DOCUMENT ASSIGNMENT

You are required to prepare the final document using your Word Processing assignment file. Recall the file and amend it as shown, incorporating the extracts you produced in the Database and Spreadsheet assignments, and the pie chart from the Graphics assignment, where indicated.

Please ensure that the format specification covers the Database and Spreadsheet extracts of your document. The graphical representation must be legible and displayed within the margins.

---

1 Recall your Word Processing assignment and use the specification shown below to produce the final document:

Top margin	Not less than 1.3 cm ($\frac{1}{2}$")	**5.4(a)**
Left margin	Not less than 1.3 cm ($\frac{1}{2}$")	**5.4(b)**
Line length	16.5 cm ($6\frac{1}{2}$")	**5.4(c)**
Line spacing	Single	**5.4(d)**
Alignment	Justified	**5.4(e)**
Character size	12 point or 12 cpi (increase size)	**5.4(h)**
Paper size	A4	**5.8(d)**
Page numbers	Bottom centre. Start at page 10.	**5.4(f) (g)**

5.1(a)

---

2 Amend your file as indicated. If necessary, resize the bar chart and repaginate. Save the amended file using a unique filename. Make a copy of your file using a unique filename, and record the details of both on the File Store Record Sheet.

5.4(i) (j) (l)
5.5(a) (b)
5.6(a)
5.7(a)

---

3 Print the document on A4 paper.

5.8(a) (b) (c)
(d) (e)

INTEGRATE FILES AND PRESENT A DOCUMENT ASSIGNMENT

Warrant No   JN24300/95

Client   JOHN WESTWOOD

Address   17 DUDLEY ROAD, RUNCORN

We attended the premises shown ~~on the warrant~~, where we obtained walking

possession.

[delete]

5.3(a)

5.3(b)

When we interviewed the owner we were informed that settlement was not

possible, but an offer to repay at £1,000.00 per month (with the first payment

immediately) was recorded.

We informed the owner that we would submit the offer to yourselves, and await

further instructions.

We look forward to hearing from you regarding this matter.

The relevant reference communications to the Under Sheriff have been

forwarded to your Chester Office.

We have made contact with the solicitors of the owner regarding the above

agreement, and they inform us that a cheque regarding the warrant has been

forwarded for direction to the warrant account.

When we receive the payment, we will forward the amount (less fees

and expenses) to the Under Sheriff's Office.

5.3(a)

5.3(b)

The following accounts are also under consideration.

~~Should there be any problems regarding this matter we will advise you accordingly.~~

[delete]

5.2(b)

> Insert the SPREADSHEET extract here, using the format specified for this document, including character size

5.4(k)

NEW PAGE

INTEGRATE FILES AND PRESENT A DOCUMENT ASSIGNMENT

MARKETING REPORT

We recognise that court costs can be a major problem. You may be surprised to learn that we can carry out court action that will result in minimal expense to the company.

We could offer this service to other companies. Using our services an enormous number of court actions have incurred no costs. The majority of cases are brought with clients repaying over 2 years. You will see from the breakdown that over 30% of our client caseload falls into this category.

Insert the PIE CHART here. Ensure it is legible and is displayed within the margins

BEFORE ACTION

We operate an all inclusive price before action. This package includes:

receiving your instructions;

writing letters;

delete

~~dealing with telephone calls from respondents and/or their solicitors;~~

dealing with correspondence;

forwarding correspondence and messages;

dealing with payments received;

a reminder service.

INTEGRATE FILES AND PRESENT A DOCUMENT ASSIGNMENT

OBJECTIVES

COURT ACTION

Quite simply, the cost of court action where the proceedings are successful can be zero. Costs are only incurred if the outstanding amount is higher than £750. The higher the outstanding amount, the lower the cost. If there are many high figure accounts, there could be greater savings. *This is the case in the Runcorn sector.*

5.3(a) (c)

MOVE

If court action is successful the costs are as follows:

OUTSTANDING AMOUNT	MAXIMUM COST
UNDER £750	£0
£750 - £2000	£60
£2000 - £3000	£55
OVER £3000	£10

5.2(a)

Insert the DATABASE extract here, using the format specified for this document including character size and line spacing

5.3(d)

*Replace the words: the owner
with the words : Mr White
throughout this document*

CLIENT DETAIL CARDS

SURNAME	BASSETT	CNO 304	WARRANT COST	3467.00
FIRST NAME	MARTIN		FEES	182.50
DATE OF BIRTH	29 – 12 – 76		TOTAL AMOUNT DUE	3649.50
ADDRESS	40 BRACKE ROAD		START DATE	30 – 10 – 94
TOWN	BOOTLE		PAYMENT YEARS	1
TELEPHONE	01229 526311		PAYMENT FREQUENCY	MONTHLY

SURNAME	DICKINSON	CNO 595	WARRANT COST	6222.50
FIRST NAME	EDWARD		FEES	327.50
DATE OF BIRTH	17 – 10 – 70		TOTAL AMOUNT DUE	6550.00
ADDRESS	2 STONEBY DRIVE		START DATE	5 – 9 – 95
TOWN	BOOTLE		PAYMENT YEARS	3
TELEPHONE	01229 279421		PAYMENT FREQUENCY	WEEKLY

SURNAME	SANDLES	CNO 175	WARRANT COST	6325.35
FIRST NAME	JOANNA		FEES	332.90
DATE OF BIRTH	23 – 12 – 66		TOTAL AMOUNT DUE	6658.25
ADDRESS	210 WARREN DRIVE		START DATE	12 – 7 – 95
TOWN	BOOTLE		PAYMENT YEARS	1
TELEPHONE	01229 396334		PAYMENT FREQUENCY	QUARTERLY

SURNAME	GRENSON CNO 661	WARRANT COST	8359.30
FIRST NAME	JOAN	FEES	440.70
DATE OF BIRTH	28 – 11 – 48	TOTAL AMOUNT DUE	8800.00
ADDRESS	9 BRADLEY PLACE	START DATE	14 – 10 – 93
TOWN	CHESTER	PAYMENT YEARS	1
TELEPHONE	01244 235660	PAYMENT FREQUENCY	WEEKLY

SURNAME	FREEMANTLE CNO 235	WARRANT COST	9380.00
FIRST NAME	PETER	FEES	492.10
DATE OF BIRTH	8 – 11 – 63	TOTAL AMOUNT DUE	9872.10
ADDRESS	41 CHESHAM ROAD	START DATE	2 – 3 – 95
TOWN	CHESTER	PAYMENT YEARS	2
TELEPHONE	01244 612599	PAYMENT FREQUENCY	QUARTERLY

SURNAME	DIXON CNO 124	WARRANT COST	6215.00
FIRST NAME	PETER	FEES	327.60
DATE OF BIRTH	7 – 1 – 63	TOTAL AMOUNT DUE	6542.60
ADDRESS	21 NEWTON ROAD	START DATE	19 – 12 – 94
TOWN	BOOTLE	PAYMENT YEARS	1
TELEPHONE	01229 651006	PAYMENT FREQUENCY	MONTHLY

CLIENT DETAIL CARDS

SURNAME	ROBERTS	CNO 495	WARRANT COST	2422 . 25
FIRST NAME	KEN		FEES	127 . 25
DATE OF BIRTH	28 – 12 – 48		TOTAL AMOUNT DUE	2549 . 50
ADDRESS	21 SHENTON STREET		START DATE	24 – 9 – 95
TOWN	RUNCORN		PAYMENT YEARS	2
TELEPHONE	01928 100921		PAYMENT FREQUENCY	WEEKLY

SURNAME	BATTY	CNO 114	WARRANT COST	6253 . 20
FIRST NAME	MELVYN		FEES	329 . 60
DATE OF BIRTH	23 – 12 – 42		TOTAL AMOUNT DUE	6582 . 80
ADDRESS	14 LAMPTON ROAD		START DATE	31 – 10 – 94
TOWN	BOOTLE		PAYMENT YEARS	1
TELEPHONE	01229 462309		PAYMENT FREQUENCY	MONTHLY

SURNAME	PHILLIPS	CNO 663	WARRANT COST	9013 . 00
FIRST NAME	AMANDA		FEES	475 . 00
DATE OF BIRTH	4 – 2 – 62		TOTAL AMOUNT DUE	9488 . 00
ADDRESS	63 LEASON PLACE		START DATE	28 – 9 – 93
TOWN	RUNCORN		PAYMENT YEARS	1
TELEPHONE	01928 379211		PAYMENT FREQUENCY	WEEKLY

SURNAME	FARRELL CNO 475	WARRANT COST	8089 . 00
FIRST NAME	DONALD	FEES	425 . 60
DATE OF BIRTH	9 — 1 — 41	TOTAL AMOUNT DUE	8514 . 60
ADDRESS	21 DERBY ROAD	START DATE	4 — 7 — 95
TOWN	BOOTLE	PAYMENT YEARS	1
TELEPHONE	01229 514230	PAYMENT FREQUENCY	MONTHLY

SURNAME	WADE CNO 275	WARRANT COST	950 . 00
FIRST NAME	SUSAN	FEES	50 . 00
DATE OF BIRTH	13 — 9 — 38	TOTAL AMOUNT DUE	1000 . 00
ADDRESS	4 MORETON WAY	START DATE	29 — 7 — 95
TOWN	RUNCORN	PAYMENT YEARS	2
TELEPHONE	01928 562234	PAYMENT FREQUENCY	WEEKLY

SURNAME	RASHID CNO 195	WARRANT COST	6177 . 50
FIRST NAME	NAZIR	FEES	325 . 00
DATE OF BIRTH	24 — 3 — 32	TOTAL AMOUNT DUE	6502 . 50
ADDRESS	33 KING STREET	START DATE	10 — 9 — 95
TOWN	CHESTER	PAYMENT YEARS	1
TELEPHONE	01244 675023	PAYMENT FREQUENCY	MONTHLY

CLIENT DETAIL CARDS

SURNAME	WHEELER CNO 662	WARRANT COST	1960 . 50
FIRST NAME	JANICE	FEES	100 . 00
DATE OF BIRTH	12 – 10 – 70	TOTAL AMOUNT DUE	2060.50
ADDRESS	10 BROOK PLACE	START DATE	10 –10 – 92
TOWN	RUNCORN	PAYMENT YEARS	1
TELEPHONE	01928 926440	PAYMENT FREQUENCY	WEEKLY

SURNAME	LEE CNO 255	WARRANT COST	6987 . 25
FIRST NAME	SHARON	FEES	367 . 75
DATE OF BIRTH	10 – 1 – 27	TOTAL AMOUNT DUE	7355 . 00
ADDRESS	20 LIVERPOOL ROAD	START DATE	22 – 5 – 95
TOWN	BOOTLE	PAYMENT YEARS	1
TELEPHONE	01229 271130	PAYMENT FREQUENCY	MONTHLY

SURNAME	HANSON CNO 684	WARRANT COST	5320 . 50
FIRST NAME	CHARLES	FEES	280 . 00
DATE OF BIRTH	23 – 4 – 23	TOTAL AMOUNT DUE	5600 . 50
ADDRESS	424 CHEYNEY ROAD	START DATE	6 – 8 – 94
TOWN	CHESTER	PAYMENT YEARS	2
TELEPHONE	01244 432901	PAYMENT FREQUENCY	MONTHLY

SURNAME	HOLMES	CNO 885	WARRANT COST	5169 . 75
FIRST NAME	CHRISTY		FEES	275 . 00
DATE OF BIRTH	6 – 12 – 17		TOTAL AMOUNT DUE	5444 . 75
ADDRESS	17 RUDGRAVE SQUARE		START DATE	8 – 8 – 95
TOWN	RUNCORN		PAYMENT YEARS	3
TELEPHONE	01928 172100		PAYMENT FREQUENCY	WEEKLY

SURNAME	THOMPSON	CNO 105	WARRANT COST	3854 . 00
FIRST NAME	CRAIG		FEES	202 . 00
DATE OF BIRTH	9 – 1 – 41		TOTAL AMOUNT DUE	4056 . 00
ADDRESS	62 CAREY STREET		START DATE	10 – 9 – 95
TOWN	BOOTLE		PAYMENT YEARS	1
TELEPHONE	01229 563324		PAYMENT FREQUENCY	MONTHLY

SURNAME	BISANDRO	CNO 294	WARRANT COST	2454 . 00
FIRST NAME	ROSA		FEES	129 . 25
DATE OF BIRTH	27 – 12 – 29		TOTAL AMOUNT DUE	2583 . 25
ADDRESS	14 VACTONE STREET		START DATE	5 – 12 – 94
TOWN	BOOTLE		PAYMENT YEARS	1
TELEPHONE	01229 832912		PAYMENT FREQUENCY	WEEKLY

CLIENT DETAIL CARDS

SURNAME	CARRASCO	CNO 714	WARRANT COST	8386 . 00
FIRST NAME	JOSEPH		FEES	440 . 70
DATE OF BIRTH	27 – 12 – 58		TOTAL AMOUNT DUE	8826 . 70
ADDRESS	29 RICE LANE		START DATE	27 – 11 – 94
TOWN	BOOTLE		PAYMENT YEARS	3
TELEPHONE	01229 940117		PAYMENT FREQUENCY	MONTHLY

SURNAME	BANCROFT	CNO 284	WARRANT COST	1900 . 50
FIRST NAME	THOMAS		FEES	100 . 00
DATE OF BIRTH	28 – 11 – 58		TOTAL AMOUNT DUE	2000 . 50
ADDRESS	46 COMELY BANK		START DATE	20 – 10 – 94
TOWN	CHESTER		PAYMENT YEARS	3
TELEPHONE	01244 505829		PAYMENT FREQUENCY	QUARTERLY

SURNAME	TOWERS	CNO 914	WARRANT COST	5214 . 00
FIRST NAME	ESTELLE		FEES	274 . 00
DATE OF BIRTH	26 – 6 – 55		TOTAL AMOUNT DUE	5488 . 00
ADDRESS	7 SANDRINGHAM ROAD		START DATE	9 – 10 – 94
TOWN	BOOTLE		PAYMENT YEARS	2
TELEPHONE	01229 562320		PAYMENT FREQUENCY	QUARTERLY

CLIENT DETAIL CARDS

SURNAME	BENSON CNO 664	WARRANT COST	6269 . 50
FIRST NAME	GRAHAM	FEES	330 . 00
DATE OF BIRTH	11 – 12 – 71	TOTAL AMOUNT DUE	6599 . 50
ADDRESS	14 CHARLOTTE ROAD	START DATE	11 – 11 – 93
TOWN	RUNCORN	PAYMENT YEARS	2
TELEPHONE	01928 711211	PAYMENT FREQUENCY	MONTHLY

SURNAME	MURRAY CNO 315	WARRANT COST	6175 . 00
FIRST NAME	STEVE	FEES	324 . 50
DATE OF BIRTH	12 – 9 – 54	TOTAL AMOUNT DUE	6499 . 50
ADDRESS	9 BUCHANON ROAD	START DATE	30 – 1 – 95
TOWN	BOOTLE	PAYMENT YEARS	1
TELEPHONE	01229 526093	PAYMENT FREQUENCY	MONTHLY

SURNAME	HOWARD CNO 355	WARRANT COST	5795 . 00
FIRST NAME	JAMES	FEES	305 . 00
DATE OF BIRTH	28 – 11 – 51	TOTAL AMOUNT DUE	6100 . 00
ADDRESS	122 WENTON WAY	START DATE	3 – 5 – 95
TOWN	BOOTLE	PAYMENT YEARS	2
TELEPHONE	01229 825100	PAYMENT FREQUENCY	QUARTERLY

Integrated Business Technology Stage II syllabus

7

| 1 | SET UP AND USE THE FACILITIES OF A DATABASE STRUCTURE |

Assessment objectives	Performance criteria
Candidates must be able to:	
1.1 SELECT the relevant data	(a) Only required data is included
1.2 ENTER the record structure	(a) Specified fields are set up (b) Field type is set appropriate to the data (numeric, alpha and date) (c) Field width is set to accommodate the specified data
1.3 ENTER the data	(a) All data entered with no more than 3 Data Entry Errors (b) Data is encoded
1.4 SEARCH on three criteria to select a subset of the data	(a) Specified selection is made of all records in subset
1.5 SORT data (alphanumeric/numeric)	(a) Data is in specified order
1.6 CREATE reports	(a) Specified report created to display all records in table format (b) Specified report created to display fields in table format (c) Report created to display fields in specified order in table format (d) Specified field headings created
1.7 SAVE data, structure, subsets and reports	(a) Structure and data of whole file is saved (b) Specified data subsets are saved to be recalled at a later date (c) Specified reports are saved to be recalled at a later date (d) Unique file names are used
1.8 RECORD file storage details	(a) File storage details are recorded
1.9 PRINT reports	(a) Specified reports are printed in table format (b) Specified field headings are printed (c) If continuous stationery is used page break does not cross perforations

2 CREATE AND USE A SPREADSHEET TO AID PROBLEM SOLVING

Assessment objectives

Performance criteria

Candidates must be able to:

2.1 SELECT the relevant data
- (a) Only required data is included

2.2 ENTER the spreadsheet layout
- (a) Cell widths are set as instructed
- (b) Text is aligned as specified
- (c) Figures are right justified
- (d) Figures are displayed in integer format unless otherwise specified
- (e) Monetary amounts are presented to 2 decimal places unless otherwise specified
- (f) Monetary amounts are displayed in sterling unless otherwise specified

2.3 ENTER text and data into the spreadsheet
- (a) Text is entered with no more than 3 Data Entry Errors
- (b) Numeric data is entered with 100% accuracy

2.4 GENERATE and APPLY formulae
- (a) Formulae are entered which generate required results
- (b) Formulae replicated as specified

2.5 INSERT a column/row
- (a) Column/row is inserted in correct position
- (b) Column/row is inserted with correct format

2.6 GENERATE projections
- (a) Correct projections are made
- (b) Text is amended

2.7 SAVE structure and data
- (a) Files are saved before and after changes as specified
- (b) Unique file names are used
- (c) Structure and data of whole file can be recalled at a later date
- (d) Specified section of spreadsheet can be recalled at a later date

2.8 RECORD file storage details
- (a) File storage details are recorded

2.9 PRINT the spreadsheet data*
- (a) Specified cells are printed
- (b) Appropriate column headings are printed
- (c) If continuous stationery is used page break does not cross perforations

2.10 PRINT spreadsheet formulae
- (a) Formulae are printed

*NOTE monetary data may be printed with or without £ sign

3 | USE WORD PROCESSING FACILITIES TO PRODUCE A MULTI-PAGE DOCUMENT

Assessment objectives	Performance criteria
Candidates must be able to:	
3.1 IMPLEMENT a document format	(a) Top margin is set as specified
	(b) Left margin is set as specified
	(c) Line length is set as specified
	(d) Line spacing is set as specified
	(e) Justification is set as specified
	(f) Character size is set as specified
	(g) Page breaks are inserted as specified
3.2 ENTER the data	(a) Text is entered with no more than 3 Data Entry Errors
3.3 USE emphasis	(a) All the portion indicated (but no more) is emphasised
3.4 USE indentation	(a) All the portion indicated (but no more) is indented
3.5 CENTRE line(s)	(a) Specified data is 'acceptably' centred (i.e. over text or on page)
3.6 PRESENT a table	(a) Data is presented in table as specified
3.7 NUMBER the pages	(a) Position of page numbers is as specified or, if not specified, anywhere above or below text
	(b) Page numbers are positioned consistently
3.8 SAVE the document	(a) Document is saved as specified
	(b) Unique file name is used
3.9 RECORD file storage details	(a) File storage details are recorded
3.10 PRINT the document	(a) Specified paper size is used
	(b) Document is legible and complete
	(c) If continuous stationery is used page break does not cross perforations

4 | PRODUCE GRAPHICAL REPRESENTATIONS OF NUMERIC DATA

4.1 SELECT the relevant data	(a) Correct data is selected
4.2 ENTER text	(a) All text entered with no more than 3 Data Entry Errors
	(b) Heading is entered as specified on bar chart
	(c) Axes labels are entered as specified on bar chart
	(d) Bar labels are entered as specified on bar chart
	(e) Heading is entered as specified on pie chart
	(f) Sector labels are entered as specified on pie chart OR legend applied
4.3 PRODUCE graphical representations	(a) Numeric data is graphed as specified with 100% accuracy
	(b) Specified scale is used
	(c) Percentage value OR numeric value of pie chart segments are displayed
4.4 SAVE the graphical representations	(a) Files are saved before and after changes as specified
	(b) Unique file name is used
	(c) Graphical representations can be recalled at a later date

Assessment objectives	Performance criteria
Candidates must be able to:	
4.5 RECORD file storage details	(a) File storage details are recorded
4.6 PRINT the graphical representations	(a) Graphical representation is printed in portrait
	(b) Graphical representation is printed in landscape
	(c) If continuous stationery is used page break does not cross perforations

5 INTEGRATE FILES AND PRESENT A DOCUMENT

5.1 RETRIEVE previously stored document	(a) Specified document is retrieved
5.2 IMPORT information according to instructions	(a) Required portion of the Database assignment is imported as specified
	(b) Required portion of the Spreadsheet assignment is imported as specified
	(c) Required portion of the Graphical Representation assignment is imported as specified
5.3 AMEND document	(a) Data is inserted as specified with no more than 3 Data Entry Errors
	(b) Data is deleted as specified
	(c) Data is moved as specified
	(d) Data is replaced as specified
5.4 FORMAT information	(a) Top margin is set as specified
	(b) Left margin is set as specified
	(c) Line length is set as specified
	(d) Line spacing is set as specified
	(e) Justification is set as specified
	(f) Page numbers are controlled
	(g) Position of page numbers is as specified or, if not specified, anywhere above or below text
	(h) Character size is set as specified
	(i) Information is presented in specified sequence
	(j) Graphical representation is re-sized
	(k) Page breaks inserted as instructed
	(l) Documents are repaginated to ensure page breaks are positioned appropriately, e.g. not after headings, not before last line of a paragraph
5.5 SAVE file	(a) Amended files are saved as specified
	(b) Unique file names are used
5.6 COPY file	(a) Copy of file is produced
5.7 RECORD file storage details	(a) File storage details are recorded
5.8 PRINT final document	(a) Final document is legible and complete
	(b) Output corresponds with requirements
	(c) Waste is minimised during production of hard copy
	(d) Specified paper size used
	(e) If continuous stationery is used page break does not cross perforations

FILE STORE RECORD SHEET

Candidate name: _____

ASSIGNMENT	STEP NO	FILENAME
Database		
Spreadsheet		
Word Processing		
Graphics		
Integration		
		COPY NAME

THIS SECTION IS FOR TUTOR USE ONLY:

The tutor should tick the assignment boxes below to indicate achievement of the Assessment Objective 'Record file storage details' for each assignment.

Database ☐   Spreadsheet ☐   Word Processing ☐   Graphics ☐   Integration ☐

I confirm that I am able to recall the student's work by use of the filenames listed above.

Tutor's signature: _____

"Mmmmmmmmmmmmmmmmm," he groaned.
"A little bit higher, please, Son."

"You're just the thing for a gorilla with an itch!"

He wriggled and tickled.
And he scritched and he scratched.
And Big Gorilla opened his eyes.

"Look what you've done,"
said Mother Gorilla.
"You've woken our son."
  Baby Gorilla dashed from
his bed and jumped on
his dad's back.

He was tired and
wet as he flopped
on his bed.

my dad

And the itch?
It was worse than before!

He washed off
the ants and the
mud and the gum.

Then wearily
walked back home.

Big Gorilla raced down to
the river and jumped right in.
He splished and he splashed,
he scritched and he scratched.

And his itch was worse than before.

"It might be the thing for an elephant," said Big Gorilla, as he ran away, "but it's definitely not for me."

. . . the anthill he'd found wasn't
old at all, it was home to an army of ants!
    They bit him and nipped him
and chased him around.

So Big Gorilla found an anthill.
He leaned
    and he rubbed,
he scritched
    and he scratched.

Then he scritched
and he scratched
some more.

But . . .

"You should try rubbing against an old anthill," said Elephant. "It's just the thing for an elephant with an *itch*."

"It might be the thing
for a lion," said Big Gorilla,
"but it's definitely not for me."

. . . the grass was too *tickly* and it stuck to his back. And his *itch* was worse than before.

So Big Gorilla found some grass.
He rolled and he tumbled,
he scritched and he scratched.

But . . .

"You should try rolling in the grass," said Lion. "It's just the thing for a lion with an *itch*."

"It might be the thing for
a hog," said Big Gorilla,
"but it's definitely not for me."

. . . the mud was too **sloppy**.
And it went in his ears.
And it went in his eyes.
And his *itch* was worse than before.

So Big Gorilla found some mud.
He wallowed and he squelched,
he scritched and he scratched.

But ...

"You should wallow in the mud,"
said Warthog, with a grunt.
"It's just the thing
for a hog with an *itch*."

"It might be the thing for you," said Big Gorilla, "but it's definitely not for me."

. . . the tree was all **gummy**
and it stuck to his fur.
And his itch was
worse than before.

So Big Gorilla wandered off to find a tree.
He wriggled and he
rubbed, he scritched
and he scratched.

But . . .

Mother Gorilla frowned and said,
"You need a scratching tree,
it's just the thing when
I have an itch. Now go away
before you wake the baby."

He danced round the room,
scritching and scratching.
He bumped into a boulder,
and knocked over a log.
But he still couldn't find the itch.

But he
just couldn't
find the spot.

Big Gorilla had an itch.
It was right in the
middle of his back.

He wriggled

and he squirmed,

he reached

and he stretched.

An Itch To Scratch

Damian Harvey
illustrated by **Lynne Chapman**

GULLANE
CHILDREN'S BOOKS

With love to Rachel, Laura and Deanna – the
best back scratchers!
D.H.

For Matthew and Georgie
L.C.

First published in Great Britain in 2005 by Gullane Children's Books
This paperback edition published 2006 by
Gullane Children's Books
185 Fleet Street, London, EC4A 2HS

2   4   6   8   10   9   7   5   3

Text © Damian Harvey 2005
Illustrations © Lynne Chapman 2005

The right of Damian Harvey and Lynne Chapman to be identified as the author and illustrator of this work
has been asserted by them in accordance with the Copyright, Designs, and Patents Act, 1988.
A CIP record for this title is available from the British Library.

ISBN: 978-1-86233-589-9

Printed and bound in China

An Itch To Scratch

7

Shocked

yikes

In my dream, my dog turned into a wolf. I felt **shocked**!

sad

jealous

shocked

upset

slobber, slobber

scared   worried   cross   mean   shy

scared

worried

cross

mean

shy

Scared

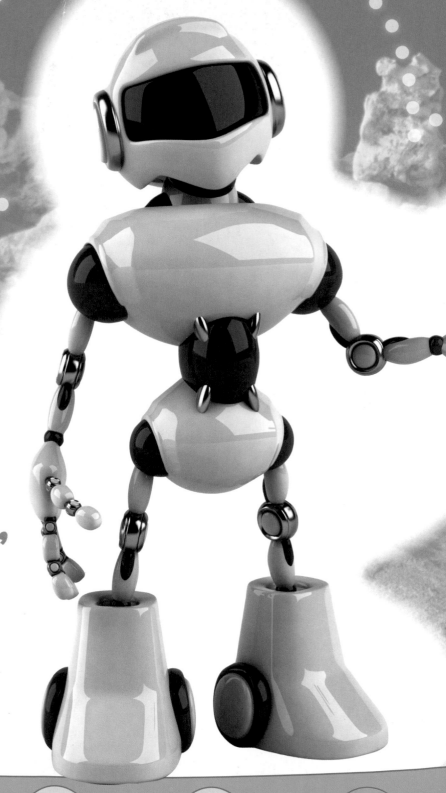

creak, creak

sad

jealous

shocked

upset

12

I dreamt about space robots.

I felt **scared**.

tremble tremble

scared · worried · cross · mean · shy

13

Worried

chatter chatter

sad

jealous

shocked

upset

Cross

I spilt water all over my picture. I felt **cross**.

sad

jealous

shocked

upset

OOOps!

splash!

scared

worried

cross

mean

shy

Mean

Waa waa!

sad   jealous   shocked   upset

18

19

21

Notes for adults

The **Feelings...** series has been designed to support and extend the learning of young children. The books link in to the Early Years curriculum and beyond. Find out more about Early Years and reading with children from the National Literacy Trust (www.literacytrust.org.uk).

The **Feelings...** series helps to develop children's knowledge, understanding and skills in key social and emotional aspects of learning (SEAL), in particular empathy, self-awareness and social skills. It aims to help children understand, articulate and manage their feelings. Visit http://nationalstrategies.standards.dcsf.gov.uk/node/87009 to find out more about SEAL.

Titles in the series:
I'm Happy and other fun feelings looks at positive emotions
I'm Sad and other tricky feelings looks at uncomfortable emotions
I'm Tired and other body feelings looks at physical feelings
I'm Busy a feelings story explores other familiar feelings

The **Feelings...** books offer the following special features:

1) **matching game**
   a border of expressive faces gives readers the chance to hunt out the face that matches the emotion covered on the spread;
2) **signing instructions**
   each spread includes clear visual instructions for signing the emotion (these follow British Sign Language standard – visit britishsignlanguage.com for more information about this organisation);
3) **fantasy scenes**
   since children often explore emotion through stories, dreams and their imaginations, two emotions (in this book, 'shocked' and 'scared') are presented in a fantasy setting, giving the opportunity to examine intense feelings in the safety of an unreal context.

Making the most of reading time
When reading with younger children, take time to explore the pictures together. Ask children to find, identify, count or describe different objects. Point out colours and textures. Pause in your reading so that children can ask questions, repeat your words or even predict the next word. This sort of participation develops early reading skills.

Follow the words with your finger as you read. The main text is in Infant Sassoon, a clear, friendly font designed for children learning to read and write. The thought and speech bubbles and sound effects add fun and give the opportunity to distinguish between levels of communication.

Extend children's learning by using this book as a springboard for discussion and follow-on activities. Here are a few ideas:

Pages 4–5: I feel sad

Make a story sack themed around losing a favourite toy. You could include *Dogger* by Shirley Hughes, *Elmer and the Lost Teddy* by David McKee and *Where's My Teddy?* by Jez Alborough. Encourage children to set up a teddy bears' picnic – they could make pretend food out of modelling dough.

Pages 6–7: I feel jealous

Talk about situations in which the children have felt jealous. What made them feel better? Discuss some strategies for joining in, instead of feeling left out.

Pages 8–9: I feel shocked

If you have a group of children, why not play 'What's the time, Mr Wolf?'. One child is Mr Wolf and stands with their back turned. The others stand at the opposite end of the room, garden or playground. Each time the children call out 'What's the time, Mr Wolf?', the wolf calls out a time between one and 12 o'clock, and the children advance that many steps. But if the wolf calls out 'Dinner time!' the children must run back to the start – if the wolf catches one, that child is the new wolf.

Pages 10–11: I feel upset

Ask children to imagine a best friend moving away. How would they stay in touch? Give each child a sheet of paper so they can 'write' a letter to this faraway friend. Divide the paper into eight. In seven of the spaces, write the day of the week, and encourage the children to draw a picture or write a few words to describe what they did on that day. In the last space, they can copy the words "What did *you* do? Love [their name]".

Pages 12–13: I feel scared

Give each child some card and felt-tips and ask them to draw the scariest monster imaginable. Help them to cut their picture into six pieces to make a jigsaw. You can make longer-lasting scary-monster jigsaws with a laminating machine.

Pages 14–15: I feel worried

Provide wooden pegs, glue and colourful scraps of cloth for making worry dolls. Worry dolls are a tradition in Guatemala. At bedtime, children tell a worry to the doll and place it under their pillow. The idea is that the doll takes care of the worry as the child sleeps (sometimes, parents take away the doll).

Pages 16–17: I feel cross

How could the girl stop feeling cross? By making an even better picture! Encourage the children to collaborate on a mural, using paints or collage materials, that shows themselves having fun.

Pages 18–19: I feel mean

Teach some noisy songs that children can sing at home in the bath – far more fun than annoying an older sibling or being mean to a younger one. 'Five little ducks' is a good one!

Pages 20–21: I feel shy

Dressing up and role play are great ways of helping children overcome their shyness. While wearing a costume, they can leave their shy self behind and become someone else – for example, a superhero or an explorer. Animal masks are a useful prop for imaginative, confidence-building play, allowing the children to practise animal moves and make appropriate noises.

23

Sign language

cross **16**

jealous **6**

mean **18**

sad **4**

scared **12**

shocked **8**

shy **20**

upset **10**

worried **14**

Index

Credits

The publisher would like to thank the following for permission to reproduce their images:
Dreamstime: cover and 4–5 (Moth), 18–19 (Cbsva);
iStockphoto: 4 (ivanastar), 6–7 (skhoward), 6 (wwing), 8–9 (AVTG), 8 basket (DNY59), 8 bone (jclegg), 10–11 (assalve), 10 (Ziva_K), 12–13 (Christian Lohman), 12bl (julos), 12c (paul geor), 14–15 (junxiao), 14 (thepalmer), 16–17 (monkeybusinessimages), 16 (piksel), 18 (jallfree), 20–21 (joelblit), 20 (markross).